HOLDEN PUBLIC LIBRARY

D0072941

REFERENCE ONLY

WITHDRAWN FROM LIBRARY

RELIGIONS
OF THE
WORLD

BUDDHISM

CHRISTIANITY

CONFUCIANISM

HINDUISM

INDIGENOUS RELIGIONS

ISLAM

JUDAISM

NEW RELIGIONS

SHINTO

SIKHISM

TAOISM

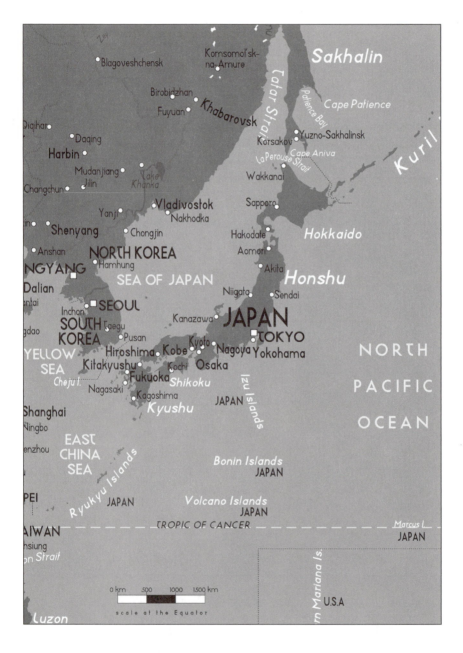

RELIGIONS
OF THE
WORLD

SHINTO

George Williams
Emeritus Professor of Religion,
California State University, Chico

Series Consulting Editor **Ann Marie B. Bahr**
Professor of Religious Studies,
South Dakota State University

Foreword by **Martin E. Marty**
Professor Emeritus,
University of Chicago Divinity School

CHELSEA HOUSE PUBLISHERS
A Haights Cross Communications Company
Philadelphia

FRONTIS: Shinto is the indigenous religion of Japan and as many as 90 percent of its 127 million people participate in some Shinto ritual practice each year.

CHELSEA HOUSE PUBLISHERS

VP, NEW PRODUCT DEVELOPMENT Sally Cheney
DIRECTOR OF PRODUCTION Kim Shinners
CREATIVE MANAGER Takeshi Takahashi
MANUFACTURING MANAGER Diann Grasse

Staff for SHINTO

EXECUTIVE EDITOR Lee Marcott
EDITOR Christian Green
PRODUCTION EDITOR Noelle Nardone
PHOTO RESEARCHER Amy Dunleavy
SERIES AND COVER DESIGNER Keith Trego
LAYOUT 21st Century Publishing and Communications, Inc.

©2005 by Chelsea House Publishers,
a subsidiary of Haights Cross Communications.
All rights reserved. Printed and bound in the United States of America.

A Haights Cross Communications ⤙ Company

www.chelseahouse.com

First Printing

9 8 7 6 5 4 3 2 1

Library of Congress Cataloging-in-Publication Data

Williams, George, 1940–
  Shinto/George Williams.
    p. cm.—(Religions of the world)
Includes bibliographical references and index.
  ISBN 0-7910-8097-8 — 0-7910-8355-1 (pbk.) ·
  1. Shinto. I. Title. II. Series.
BL2220.W55 2004
299.561—dc22
                                              2004011863

All links and web adresses were checked and verified to be correct at the time of publication. Because of the dynamic nature of the web, some addresses and links may have changed since publication and may no longer be valid.

CONTENTS

Foreword

Martin E. Marty

On this very day, like all other days, hundreds of millions of people around the world will turn to religion for various purposes.

On the one hand, there are purposes that believers in any or all faiths, as well as unbelievers, might regard as positive and benign. People turn to religion or, better, to their own particular faith, for the experience of healing and to inspire acts of peacemaking. They want to make sense of a world that can all too easily overwhelm them because it so often seems to be meaningless and even absurd. Religion then provides them with beauty, inspires their souls, and impels them to engage in acts of justice and mercy.

To be informed citizens of our world, readers have good reason to learn about these features of religions that mean so much to so many. Those who study the faiths do not have to agree with any of them and could not agree with all of them, different as they are. But they need basic knowledge of religions to understand other people and to work out strategies for living with them.

On the other hand—and religions always have an "other hand"—believers in any of the faiths, and even unbelievers who are against all of them, will find their fellow humans turning to their religions for purposes that seem to contradict all those positive features. Just as religious people can heal and be healed, they can also kill or be killed in the name of faith. So it has been through history.

This killing can be literal: Most armed conflicts and much terrorism today are inspired by the stories, commands, and promises that come along with various faiths. People can and do read and act upon scriptures that can breed prejudice and that lead them to reject other beliefs and believers. Or the killing can be figurative, which means that faiths can be deadening to the spirit. In the name of faith, many people are repressed, oppressed, sometimes victimized and abused.

If religion can be dangerous and if it may then come with "Handle with Care" labels, people who care for their own security, who want to lessen tensions and inspire concord, have to equip themselves by learning something about the scriptures and stories of their own and other faiths. And if they simply want to take delight in human varieties and imaginings, they will find plenty to please them in lively and reliable accounts of faiths.

A glance at television or at newspapers and magazines on almost any day will reveal stories that display one or both sides of religion. However, these stories usually have to share space with so many competing accounts, for example, of sports and enter-tainment or business and science, that writers and broadcasters can rarely provide background while writing headlines. Without such background, it is hard to make informed judgments.

The series RELIGIONS OF THE WORLD is designed to provide not only background but also rich illustrative material about the foreground, presenting the many features of faiths that are close at hand. Whoever reads all the volumes in the series will find that these religions have some elements in common. Overall, one can deduce that their followers take certain things with ultimate seriousness: human dignity, devotion to the sacred, the impulse to live a moral life. Yet few people are inspired by religions in general. They draw strength from what they hold particularly. These particulars of each faith are not always contradictory to those of others, but they are different in important ways. It is simply a fact that believers are informed and inspired by stories told in separate and special ways.

A picture might make all this vivid: Reading about a religion, visiting a place of worship, or coming into the company of those who believe in and belong to a particular faith, is like entering a room. Religions are, in a sense, spiritual "furnished apartments." Their adherents have placed certain pictures on the wall and moved in with their own kind of furnishings, having developed their special ways of receiving or blocking out light from such places. Some of their figurative apartments are airy, and some stress strength and security.

Philosopher George Santayana once wrote that, just as we do not speak language, we speak particular languages, so we have religion not as a whole but as religions "in particular." The power of each living and healthy religion, he added, consists in "its special and surprising message and in the bias which that revelation gives to life." Each creates "another world to live in."

The volumes in this series are introductions to several spiritual furnished apartments, guides to the special and surprising messages of these large and complex communities of faith, or religions. These are not presented as a set of items in a cafeteria line down which samplers walk, tasting this, rejecting that, and moving on. They are not bids for window-shoppers or shoppers of any sort, though it may be that a person without faith might be drawn to one or another expression of the religions here described. The real intention of the series is to educate.

Education could be dull and drab. Picture a boring professor standing in front of a class and droning on about distant realities. The authors in this series, however, were chosen because they can bring readers up close to faiths and, sometimes better, to people of faith; not to religion but to people who are religious in particular ways.

As one walks the streets of a great metropolis, it is not easy and may not even be possible to deduce the faith-commitments of those one passes unless they wear a particular costume— some garb or symbol prescribed by their faith. Therefore, while passing them by, it is not likely that one can learn much about the dreams and hopes, the fears and intentions, of those around them.

These books, in effect, stop the procession of passersby and bid visitors to enter those sanctuaries where communities worship. Each book could serve as a guide to worship. Several years ago, a book called *How to Be a Perfect Stranger* offered brief counsel on how to feel and to be at home among worshipers from other traditions. This series recognizes that we are not strangers to each other only in sanctuaries. We carry over our attachments to conflicting faiths where we go to work or vote or serve in the military or have fun. These "carryovers" tend to come from the basic stories and messages of the several faiths.

The publishers have taken great pains to assign their work to authors of a particular sort. Had these been anti-religious or anti–the religion about which they write, they would have done a disservice. They would, in effect, have been blocking the figurative doors to the faiths or smashing the furniture in the sanctuaries. On the other hand, it would be wearying and distorting had the assignment gone to public relations agents, advertisers who felt called to claim "We're Number One!" concerning the faith about which they write.

Fair-mindedness and accuracy are the two main marks of these authors. In rather short compass, they reach a wide range of subjects, focusing on everything one needs to advance basic understanding. Their books are like mini-encyclopedias, full of information. They introduce the holidays that draw some neighbors to be absent from work or school for a day or a season. They include galleries of notable figures in each faith-community.

Since most religions in the course of history develop different ways in the many diverse places where they thrive, or because they attract intelligent, strong-willed leaders and writers, they come up with different emphases. They divide and split off into numberless smaller groups: Protestant and Catholic and Orthodox Christians, Shiite and Sunni Muslims, Orthodox and Reform Jews, and many kinds of Buddhists and Hindus. The writers in this series do justice to these variations, providing a kind of map without which one will get lost in the effort to understand.

Some years ago, a rabbi friend, Samuel Sandmel, wrote a book about his faith called *The Enjoyment of Scripture*. What an astonishing concept, some might think: After all, religious scriptures deal with desperately urgent, life-and-death-and-eternity issues. They have to be grim and those who read them likewise. Not so. Sandmel knew what the authors of this series also know and impart: the journeys of faith and the encounter with the religions of others include pleasing and challenging surprises. I picture many a reader coming across something on these pages that at first looks obscure or forbidding, but then, after a slightly longer look, makes sense and inspires an "aha!" There are many occasions for "aha-ing!" in these books. One can also wager that many a reader will come away from the encounters thinking, "I never knew that!" or "I never thought of that before." And they will be more ready than they had been to meet strangers of other faiths in a world that so many faiths *have* to share, or that they *get* to share.

Martin E. Marty
The University of Chicago

Preface

Ann Marie B. Bahr

The majority of people, both in the United States and around the world, consider religion to be an important part of their lives. Beyond its significance in individual lives, religion also plays an important role in war and peace, politics, social policy, ethics, and cultural expression. Yet few people feel well-prepared to carry on a conversation about religion with friends, colleagues, or their congressional delegation. The amount of knowledge people have about their own faith varies, but very few can lay claim to a solid understanding of a religion other than their own. As the world is drawn closer together by modern communications, and the religions of the world jostle each other in religiously plural societies, the lack of our ability to dialogue about this aspect of our lives results in intercultural conflict rather than cooperation. It means that individuals of different religious persuasions will either fight about their faiths or avoid the topic of religion altogether. Neither of these responses aids in the building of healthy, religiously plural societies. This gap in our knowledge is therefore significant, and grows increasingly more significant as religion plays a larger role in national and international politics.

The authors and editors of this series are dedicated to the task of helping to prepare present and future decision-makers to deal with religious pluralism in a healthy way. The objective scholarship found in these volumes will blunt the persuasive power of popular misinformation. The time is short, however. Even now, nations are dividing along religious lines, and "neutral" states as well as partisan religious organizations are precariously, if not always intentionally, tipping delicate balances of power in favor of one religious group or another with doles of aid and support for certain policies or political leaders. Intervention in the affairs of other nations is always a risky business, but doing it without understanding of the religious sensitivities of the populace dramatically increases the chances that even well-intentioned intervention will be perceived as political coercion or cultural invasion. With such signs of ignorance already manifest, the day of reckoning for educational policies that ignore the study of the world's religions cannot be far off.

This series is designed to bring religious studies scholarship to the leaders of today and tomorrow. It aims to answer the questions that students, educators, policymakers, parents, and citizens might have about the new religious milieu in which we find ourselves. For example, a person hearing about a religion that is foreign to him or her might want answers to questions like these:

- How many people believe in this religion? What is its geographic distribution? When, where, and how did it originate?

- What are its beliefs and teachings? How do believers worship or otherwise practice their faith?

- What are the primary means of social reinforcement? How do believers educate their youth? What are their most important communal celebrations?

- What are the cultural expressions of this religion? Has it inspired certain styles of art, architecture, literature, or music? Conversely, does it avoid art, literature, or music for religious reasons? Is it associated with elements of popular culture?

- How do the people who belong to this religion remember the past? What have been the most significant moments in their history?

- What are the most salient features of this religion today? What is likely to be its future?

We have attempted to provide as broad coverage as possible of the various religious forces currently shaping the planet. Judaism, Christianity, Islam, Hinduism, Buddhism, Confucianism, Taoism, Sikhism, and Shinto have each been allocated an entire volume. In recognition of the fact that many smaller ancient and new traditions also exercise global influence, we present coverage of some of these in two additional volumes titled "Tribal Religions" and "New Religions." Each volume in the series discusses demographics and geography, founder or foundational period, scriptures, worldview, worship or practice, growing up in the religion, cultural expressions, calendar and holidays, history, and the religion in the world today.

The books in this series are written by scholars. Their approach to their subject matter is neutral and objective. They are not trying to convert readers to the religion they are describing. Most scholars, however, value the religion they have chosen to study, so you can expect the general tone of these books to be appreciative rather than critical.

Religious studies scholars are experts in their field, but they are not critics in the same sense in which one might be an art, film, or literary critic. Religious studies scholars feel obligated to describe a tradition faithfully and accurately, and to interpret it in a way that will allow nonbelievers as well as believers to grasp its essential structure, but they do not feel compelled to pass judgment on it. Their goal is to increase knowledge and understanding.

Academic writing has a reputation for being dry and uninspiring. If so, religious studies scholarship is an exception. Scholars of religion have the happy task of describing the words and deeds of some of the world's most amazing people: founders, prophets, sages, saints, martyrs, and bodhisattvas.

The power of religion moves us. Today, as in centuries past, people thrill to the ethical vision of Confucianism, or the dancing beauty of Hinduism's images of the divine. They are challenged by the one, holy God of the Jews, and comforted by the saving promise of Christianity. They are inspired by the stark purity of

Islam, by the resilience of tribal religions, by the energy and innovation of the new religions. The religions have retained such a strong hold on so many people's lives over such a long period of time largely because they are unforgettable.

Religious ideas, institutions, and professions are among the oldest in humanity's history. They have outlasted the world's great empires. Their authority and influence have endured far beyond that of Earth's greatest philosophers, military leaders, social engineers, or politicians. It is this that makes them so attractive to those who seek power and influence, whether such people intend to use their power and influence for good or evil. Unfortunately, in the hands of the wrong person, religious ideas might as easily be responsible for the destruction of the world as for its salvation. All that stands between us and that outcome is the knowledge of the general populace. In this as in any other field, people must be able to critically assess what they are being told.

The authors and editors of this series hope that all who seek to wield the tremendous powers of religion will do so with unselfish and noble intent. Knowing how unlikely it is that that will always be the case, we seek to provide the basic knowledge necessary to critically assess the degree to which contemporary religious claims are congruent with the history, scriptures, and genius of the traditions they are supposed to represent.

Ann Marie B. Bahr
South Dakota State University

1

Introduction

Of old, Heaven and Earth were not yet separated,
and the In and Yo not yet divided.
They formed a chaotic mass ...
The purer and clearer part was thinly drawn out,
and formed Heaven, while the heavier and
grosser element settled down and became Earth.

—*Nihonshoki*, Book I

A llow me to begin my introduction to Shinto by introducing a man I consider to be Shinto's most significant modern-day hero and prophet:

UNLIKELY REFORMER

Yukitaka Yamamoto (1923–2002) was born into one of Japan's oldest priestly families. He would become the ninety-sixth genera-tion of Yamamotos to be the chief priest of Tsubaki Grand Shrine in central Japan.

His father did not choose him to be a Shinto priest, but rather told him to find another profession. So he studied industrial and economic development and languages for work in Japan's newly acquired colonies. He had just turned eighteen in 1942, and had been taught to "Be prepared for sacrifice . . . ," i.e., to be prepared for the possibility that he would not return to Japan alive. He believed in the task of liberating former Western colonies in Asia and making them a part of the Co-Prosperity Spheres of Greater East Asia (ruled by Japan). Although his father was a famous pacifist, Yamamoto and his three brothers enlisted. His elder brother and twin, both of whom had been selected to become Shinto priests, died in the war.

Yamamoto enlisted in the Japanese Navy as a political officer. He arrived in the New Britain island of Rabaul, east of New Guinea, just as the war effort turned against Japan. He had been trained to improve living standards in the colonies and to work as a cultural officer and translator, but instead he saw the inhumanities of war. In March 1944, he was among the fifteen thousand Japanese soldiers who retreated to Northeast New Guinea and fled into its dense jungles. He would later write: "Coming face to face with the sufferings and privations of war is the best source of motivation to seek peace if you ask yourself honestly to what set of circumstances war is a reasonable alternative."[1] He described the many horrors of war experienced by himself and his comrades: "We survived native darts, American shells, poisonous fruits and berries, crocodiles, cannibals among our own, hostile Japanese units, a merciless jungle and our own doubts and fears and anxieties."[2]

After 550 days he emerged from the jungle and surrendered to U.S. soldiers, months after the end of the war. Upon returning to Japan he was asked by his father to become a Shinto priest, but he felt so impure that he turned to Shinto practice—not study for the priesthood—to heal himself. Each night for ten years, no matter how bitter the winter or how he felt physically, he performed an ancient ritual of purification called misogi, *bathing in an icy waterfall. He emerged from this period prepared, not by his own design, to become his father's successor and Shrine Shinto's great reformer. (More about Rev. Yamamoto's life later . . .)*

SIZE AND DISTRIBUTION

Shinto is the indigenous religious tradition of Japan—at least, from the point of view of the majority culture.[3] It is an ethnic religion, meaning that it is associated almost exclusively with Japan and the Japanese people. Only a very few forms of Shinto seek converts or engage in missionary work, and these few are probably better classified as "new religions" than as Shinto proper.

Shinto is so closely allied with the land and people of Japan that it is impossible to imagine Japan without Shinto, or Shinto without Japan. Shinto is not a universalizing faith, that is, it does not seek to extend its influence to all corners of the globe. Rather, Shinto discovers the sacred in the landscape of Japan, in the ancestors of Japanese families, and in the heroes associated with that one nation. Among the major Western religions, Shinto is most like Judaism, because it is associated with a single people and a particular land. But in other ways, as we shall see, it differs from Judaism.

Does everyone in Japan practice Shinto? That question is harder to answer than it seems. First, there is no Shinto equivalent of membership.[4] And second, there is confusion about what belonging to Shinto would mean.

People are generally born into Shinto when they are born Japanese. All Japanese participate in Shinto to the extent that Shinto shapes Japanese culture. But when Japanese people are asked if they are a member of Shinto, the majority say they are not. Japanese people avoid making such an assertion because it would mean that they are a Shinto professional—a priest or priestess. Even after the intended meaning of the question is carefully explained, only about thirty percent of the population of Japan will claim that Shinto is their religion.

In the first part of the twentieth century, being a loyal citizen of Japan implied practicing Shinto. But after World War II, the situation changed. Separation of church and state was forced upon Japan. Since that time, Japanese people more easily exclude themselves from any formal affiliation with Shinto.

Since there is no ritual for becoming a member of Shinto, one could perhaps count "Shinto members" by including those persons that join certain specified Shinto organizations. Even then, however, the idea of being a member of Shinto is strange. Most Japanese never ask that question of themselves. What we *can* say is that as many as 90 percent of the population of Japan (the population of Japan is approximately 127 million) are involved in some Shinto ritual practice each year; for example, attending the New Year's ritual or going to a wedding at a Shinto Shrine. These Shinto activities are so much a part of the culture that they are usually not separated out as being religious activities.

The Japanese word for "religion" (*shûkyô*) is quite recent and is thought to imply dogma. Since Japanese people generally do not want to be considered dogmatic, only about ten percent would say they are "religious" in the sense of "dogmatic." (Some, however, would be polite and answer what they think the questioner wishes to hear!) Yet, paradoxically, if one adds up the various activities Japanese people attend and the events they involve themselves in at Buddhist temples and Shinto shrines, the percentage of the population that participates in religious activities often tops 130 percent! What this tells us is that many people are involved in religious activities in both Shinto and Buddhist traditions (and many are involved in Christian events as well), but they are not comfortable identifying themselves as "religious" if they perceive that to mean espousing exclusive membership or dogmatic confessions of belief. I will have much to say later about "action-centered" religion—religion that is centered on doing and acting rather than believing or confessing. For now, let it suffice to say that Shinto is an action-centered religion (one based on actions) and not a confessional religion (one that requires a set of beliefs or a profession of faith). Since the vast majority of Japanese people are involved in Shinto rituals and festivals, it seems safe to say that Shinto includes most of Japan's population in a loose and almost unconscious way. For most people, Shinto is not a deliberate choice or a conscious commitment, but something deeper than that. While joining individual religious organizations may be a matter of individual choice, "joining Shinto" does not need to be a matter of rational choice because it is of the essence of what it means to be Japanese.

Among American Protestants who are used to stressing the importance of individual commitment this loose and almost unconscious sense of belonging will almost certainly be seen as a weakness, but that is to misunderstand Shinto. While the Protestant emphasis on repentance and conversion seeks to draw people out of a sinful world and into a right relationship with God, Shinto seeks to shape right relationships with the sacred from birth to death and beyond, never allowing the individual to depart from "the Way." (Later chapters will explore the major concepts of action-centered religion, ritual encoding of ethics, and Shinto usage of rituals.)

THE UNIQUENESS OF SHINTO

Unlike the major Western religions (Judaism, Christianity, and Islam), Shinto has no historical founder; its roots lie deep in the prehistoric religious practices of the Japanese people. Shinto has no ritual of membership or conversion, since it is assumed that birth brings one into its fold. Shinto also has no Bible—no canon of sacred scriptures; yet it has sacred books. It has no revealed code of ethics or moral commandments; yet Shinto does have a moral system encoded in its rituals. (While each of these characterizations is correct for "mainstream" Shinto, there are exceptions.)

Shinto does not fit into comparative categories easily. In some ways it is more like Native American religions or ancient Hawaiian religion than it is like Christianity or Islam. Around the world, these indigenous religions were considered primitive and nearly obliterated. Shinto, an indigenous religion that came into historical view as a tribal or clan religion, survived and developed into a religion that defines an entire civilization.

In spite of Japan's longstanding contact with the Western world, and its high degree of modernization, Shinto remains resistant to Western modes of analysis. Take, for instance, its concept of the divine. Shinto's concept of divinity has been described as animistic by some, polytheistic by others, and even "dualistic monism" by one writer.[5] Each of these categories catches something of Shinto at one point in its development, or describes one emphasis among others, but each fails as a comprehensive description. Other categories used by Western scholars that do not work for all the varieties of Shinto are the following: transcendent (beyond our senses and knowledge), scriptural (based on a holy book), universalizing (striving to exist everywhere), personal (based on a personal relationship with a personal God), and confessional or doctrinal (based on acceptance of a set of beliefs).[6] Shinto stands apart from Western religions. Therefore, understanding Shinto will involve an expansion of ideas about religion to include the aspects of religion that Shinto has developed. It will also require an approach to understanding that does not need simple answers framed in simplistic models. The effort will be richly rewarded, for there is no way to understand Japanese history and civilization without an adequate grounding in Shinto.

EXAMPLES OF BIASED SCHOLARSHIP

Some very intelligent people have misjudged Shinto, largely because they lacked the interpretive framework that this book seeks to provide. Consider, for example, the following words of Sir Charles Eliot, written shortly before World War II (note how dated and judgmental his interpretation of Shinto was):

> It is strange that this ancient ceremonial paganism should have survived among an unusually intelligent and progressive race. It is not even artistic, for it worships no images . . . It has no moral code; its prayers and sacrifices aim at obtaining temporal prosperity and indicate no desire for moral or spiritual blessings . . . So primitive is the thought of Shinto that it is hardly correct to say that natural features or individuals are deified. They are simply accepted as important facts in the continuous national life . . .[7]

Sir Charles' negative judgments do not stand alone. Two decades later another Western scholar, William Aston, stated: "It is difficult to augur a great future for Shinto. Especially when stripped of Buddhist and Chinese accretions, it is far too rudimentary a cult to satisfy the spiritual and moral wants of a nation that has a pinch of enlightenment and civilization."[8]

Will Durant, a noted historian, wrote in *Our Oriental Heritage*: "Shinto required no creed, no elaborate ritual, no moral code; it had no special priesthood, and no consoling doctrine of immortality and heaven; all that it asked of its devotee was an occasional pilgrimage, and pious reverence for one's ancestors, the emperor, and the past. It was for a time superseded because it was too modest in its rewards and demands."[9]

Pages later Durant charged that Shinto was a primary cause of Japanese militarism.[10] The comments of Eliot, Aston, and Durant reflect the superiority complex that Westerners assumed toward the rest of the world in the nineteenth and twentieth centuries. Too many Western scholars shared this condescending attitude, making Western categories for interpreting religions biased against non-Western religions in general and Shinto in particular.

Even famed Japanese Buddhist D.T. Suzuki contributed to the confusion about Shinto. He suggested that the religious insights of other traditions are not found in Shinto, simply because its nature is too emotional and sensory to be very spiritual.[11]

Unfortunately, too many modern writers repeat these old charges against Shinto in their works on Japanese subjects. It is easy to find negative assessments of Shinto; assessments based on inaccurate information and dated interpretations.

WESTERN MODELS FOR CATEGORIZING RELIGION

Scholars of religion seek to understand how different religions apprehend the sacred. Before we describe the way in which Shinto apprehends the sacred, let us look at some of the categories that shaped past comparisons. The following table outlines the

ALLEGED SHORTCOMINGS OF SHINTO

Primitive
Not intellectually interesting
No scripture
No ethical code
No creed
No special priesthood
No absolute deity
Not really spiritual
Neither funerals nor a real heaven
Militaristic, nationalistic

(This list is only suggestive—it is not exhaustive!)

Until just recently these allegations have been repeated in encyclopedia articles, popular books, and even older "authoritative studies." Each allegation reflects a conclusion from an "outside point of view"— an *etic* viewpoint—with whatever "truth" that viewpoint might contain. But the danger of an etic view is that the comparison might not be appropriate. It could be just another comparison of apples and oranges. The insiders' points of view (and there are always many) are difficult to understand without comparisons with what is familiar. These *emic* viewpoints are now balanced with etic comparisons to attain a more balanced understanding.

differences between Shinto and an idealized modern Western religion (the idealized modern Western religion is a composite of contemporary Jewish, Christian, and Islamic traits):

SHINTO WORLDVIEW	MODERN WESTERN RELIGIOUS WORLDVIEW
Experiential	Doctrinal, confessional
Mythic, mythological	Historical, scriptural
Immanent (sacred *within* the world)	Transcendent (sacred *beyond* the world)
Relative truth	Absolute truth
Communal personhood and ethics	Individual personhood and ethics
Native, ethnic, tribal	Universalizing
Identity in clan or nation	Identity in self
Action-centered	Belief-centered
Sacred time: cyclic	Sacred time: eschatological
Sacred community: immanent nation and ruler	Sacred community: transcendent symbol of grace and redemption

CATEGORIES USED TO COMPARE SHINTO AND WESTERN RELIGIONS
Experiential

Shinto proposes no set of doctrines, no confession or creed, that one must accept in order to be considered "orthodox." There is no concept of orthodoxy in Shinto.[12] This is not, as some have thought, a sign that Shinto is primitive and nonrational. What Shinto assumes is a world in which the sacred can be *experienced*. Furthermore, what is experienced is not a symbol or sign that points *beyond* itself to something supernatural, but rather something that has the sacred *within* it.[13] The object in which the sacred is experienced is called *kami*. (We will learn more about kami in the next chapter.) Generally, kami-ness was discovered in things within nature that were unusual, extraordinary, powerful, awesome; even a little frightening. All of these attributes were used by Rudolf Otto in his description of the "holy" or *mysterium tremendum*.[14] For the early Japanese, something that had kami-ness would exhibit an unusual amount of power (*ki*) or purity (*harai*). The determination of whether something was kami or not was based on human experience, and validated by the community, either by the clan in the case of a clan kami (*ujigami*), or by priests. Priests had the task of enshrining the kami in Shrine Shinto.[15]

Mircea Eliade called the appearance of the sacred a "hierophany,"[16] from the Greek words for "sacred" and "manifestation." Eliade contrasted the "sacred" with the "profane" or mundane (the ordinary). His description works for Shinto with one *proviso*: Shinto views the profane or ordinary world as having insufficient power (ki) or purity (harai) to be kami, but everything in nature is endowed with at least a small portion of nature's highest or central qualities. In Shinto the ordinary is not evil. Everything has a little ki and can be purified.

Mythic, Mythological

The written scriptures of Judaism, Christianity, and Islam are believed to contain the revealed word of God. Insofar as the Bible or the Qur'an tells the history of specific people or groups of people, each is believed to be historically accurate. Myth is often oral, and appears to contain highly imaginary tales. Initially, then, it appears that the widest possible gap should exist between scripture and history on the one hand, and myth and story on the other. That is why scholars thought it would be much easier to separate myth from scripture than has turned out to be the case.

Myth is a story that transmits a culture by informing its hearers about the nature of the world, and about the right way to relate to all that lives in it. Scriptures, too, inform people about the nature of the world and the right way to live in it. Mythic stories and scriptural stories are both interpreted anew in each generation. They are not "dead history," but "living history." While the stories or the literal words on the page may remain the same, the interpretations of both myth and scripture change over the centuries, as people adapt it to their lives.

Hence the absolute distinction between scripture and myth has collapsed for all, save fundamentalists.[17] Myth is a narrative form, like storytelling, that attempts to point to the experience of the sacred or holy using linguistic and cultural forms that the audience will understand. We will explore Shinto's myths in chapter three.

Immanent

Transcendent religions (e.g., Judaism, Christianity, and Islam) have a God who is above nature, separate from it, and holds the absolute origin of the world as its first cause and creator. Shinto does not have such a concept of "God."[18] This raises the question for some of whether or not a nontranscendent religion should be considered a religion at all. In response, one might ask why transcendent religions should be privileged. The existence of "ultimate concern" has been widely recognized as a deciding characteristic of religion, and it is possible to find an ultimate concern in immanent religions as well as in transcendent religions.[19] Therefore, I contend, immanent religions are to be accepted as religions and studied without prejudgment.

Stated from the point of view of Shinto, the divine or sacred is found within nature, not above, outside or beyond it. This is why Shinto is classified as an immanent religion. The notion of immanence will be further explored as we try to understand the nature of kami in chapter two.

Relative Truth

The question of whether Shinto proposes the existence of absolute truth in addition to relative truth will be treated indirectly, since this only became an issue in philosophical Shinto schools in the nineteenth century. Shinto's notion of truth has been pragmatic, liturgical, and ritualistic. It has no words or doctrines received directly from an absolute God or contained in infallible scripture.

Relativism only became a problem during the rise and practice of State Shinto. Claims for an absolute and divine ruler on earth presupposed an absolutist foundation for the state and its ally, State Shinto. It is paradoxical how an immanent religion would meet this state need. Our discussion of this topic will be taken up again in the next two chapters on sacred sound and on sacred stories.

Communal Personhood and Ethics

The modern Western world saw a growing emphasis on the significance and importance of individual as versus corporate identity. Because Shinto did not participate in this trend, it is classified by many as "premodern" in its understanding of personhood and ethics. This privileging of Western views begs the question of whether all cultures can and/or should follow the Western trajectory. Not only Shinto, but many other indigenous cultures as well,[20] are familiar with Western individualism but prefer to maintain their communal sense of personhood and ethics. Perhaps understanding the self as realized in community is archaic rather than modern, but who is to say that makes it wrong? Shinto's communal sense of self and ethics will be studied in the chapters on sacred action and sacred ruler.

Native, Ethnic, Tribal

Shinto is classified as Japan's indigenous religion, meaning that it is native to Japan. Its origins are prior to recorded history. (It should be noted that there were other ancient, prehistoric traditions in Japan, including those of native peoples like the Ainu.)[21] It is distinguished from universalizing religions in that it has been a tradition just for the Japanese; at least up until the modern period. Native or ethnic traditions generally do not convert outsiders to their faith. One is born into it—or may marry into it. When Japan entered an imperial stage in the modern period, and Shinto was transformed into State Shinto, the problematic of native versus universalizing came to the fore. We will return to this problematic in the discussions about the sacred community.

Action-Centered

Shinto is so different from religions that are belief-centered that early scholars thought Shinto was too primitive to be a real religion. Even today you can ask a Shinto priest about almost anything ranging from rituals to ideas about the afterlife, and you will be surprised how little substance will be given as an answer. Those who practice Shinto do not feel that beliefs adequately express their faith. Shinto is founded in experience, as stated above. Of course, all religions are founded in experience. But is there something different about a faith that refuses to set up a doctrinal standard? One reason for this refusal in Shinto is its foundation in acting or doing (ritual disciplines and practices), rather than devotion (emotions of love and grace), or thinking (explanations, beliefs, doctrines, professions). This aspect of Shinto will be explored indirectly in the chapters on sacred stories and on sacred action.

Cyclic Time

The sense of time in Judaism, Christianity, and Islam is eschatological. It focuses on the belief that the world will one day come to an end, and be followed by an afterlife. Shinto's experience of sacred time is interestingly different from that found in the major Western religions. First, there is mythological time. Then, there is a notion of time as now, even an "eternal now" and an "eternal return" to a past that is again present.[22] Shinto is almost without any teachings about an afterlife or heaven. Shinto's notion of sacred time will be further explained in chapter six, where we will discuss Shinto's festivals and holidays.

Sacred Community

In the Christian worldview, the sacred community is composed of those who have been saved, and those who have been saved come from various ethnic and national backgrounds. Thus, for Christians, sacred community is not found within the parameters of an actual nation. It is a transcendent symbol of grace and redemption. In Shinto, the sacred community *is* ethnically and nationally defined, giving the Shinto community a sense of concreteness. Shinto is embedded in a particular geographic locality, and its sense of sacred community is bounded by the borders of that geographic locality.

Japan's notions of sacred community and sacred person became problematic in the modern era, when earlier ideas about identity were transformed into religious ideologies of racial superiority and reverence for the Japanese emperor (*Tennô*). These modern notions of a sacred community and its sacred leader were used to support total obedience to the imperial state. Religion and state were combined in new ways and the result was State Shinto. This discussion will be continued in the chapters on sacred story and sacred ruler.

SHINTO'S UNITY AND DIVERSITY

Having looked at some of the comparative categories applied to Shinto by its "outside" interpreters, let us turn now to the main concepts used "inside" the tradition to define Shinto. We will focus first on terms that suggest the unity of Shinto, and then on terms that describe Shinto's diversity.

SHINTO OR "KAMI NO MICHI" AS ONE TRADITION

Our first clue in understanding Shinto as a unity comes from its name: *shin* + *to*. The word "Shinto" has been created in English from oral Japanese, spelling the way the word sounds in Roman letters. In Japanese, it is much more complicated. "Shinto" is the Chinese (or *on*) reading of two Chinese characters: *shen* in Chinese (pronounced *shin* in Japanese) and *dao* in Chinese (*to* in Japanese). The Japanese (or *kun*) reading of the two characters (plus the particle *no*) is *kami no michi*. Since oral Japanese is generally polysyllabic and involves an entirely different grammatical system, the writing system from China did not work very well. Two more writing systems were developed to accommodate Japanese sounds— one for foreign words (*katakana*) and the other for Japanese words (*hiragana*).[23]

Both Shinto and kami no michi mean the "way of the kami." The ancient Chinese thought that Japanese indigenous religion was like their devotional Daoism (also transliterated Taoism), because devotional Daoists worshipped divinities (called *shen* in Chinese, *shin* in Japanese) that seemed like the Japanese kami. The Chinese word *Shen* thus acquired a second reading in Japan—kami.

In Japanese, kami is both singular and plural.[24] The kami are the innumerable Japanese deities including full-fledged divinities (such as the Sun Goddess Amaterasu, from whom the imperial family is said to descend), the divinized souls of great persons (warriors, leaders, poets, scholars), the ancestral divinities of clans (*uji*), the spirits of specific places that are often places of great natural beauty (woods, trees, springs, rocks, mountains), or the more abstract forces of nature (fertility, growth, production). Kami are generally worshipped at shrines (*jinja*—deity dwellings), which were established in their honor, and which house the sacred objects (*goshintai*) onto which the kami are said to descend.

The use of the word "Shinto" to designate a religion different from other religions did not develop until after Chinese culture, language, and religion impacted Japan in the seventh century C.E. In this sense of the term, Shinto designated a religion distinct from Chinese and Korean Buddhism, Daoism (Taoism), Confucianism, and later, in the sixteenth century, from Christianity. But one word for an entire Japanese religious tradition cannot hide the fact that Shinto is complicated and there are many varieties of Shinto, not just one.

SIX EXPRESSIONS INDICATING SHINTO'S DIVERSITY

There are at least six major expressions of Shinto: Imperial Shinto, National or State Shinto, Shrine Shinto, Sectarian Shinto, Folk or Shamanic Shinto, and Dual Shinto. These aspects are illustrated by the graphic on page 18 and show something of Shinto's variety and dynamism, as well as the overlapping of one aspect with another.

(1) **Shinto of the Imperial House** or **Imperial Shinto** (*Kôshitsu Shinto*) can be divided into two kinds. One kind continues today as the special Shinto practices at the three shrines within the grounds of the imperial palace. During imperial weddings and funerals, the public can now get a glimpse of the ancient, secret rituals performed at these shrines. While they may appear to be much like Shinto rituals performed at other shrines around Japan, the differences are significant. They are also secret in the sense that no explanations will be given beyond the imperial household.

The second kind of Imperial Shinto was largely political. In the context of Japanese religion, political meant religio-political because religion and politics were mingled. The emperor was considered divine,[25] and served as the high priest for the entire nation at special times of the year. He was the focus of patriotic duty and loyalty. When Japan's ancient military, the *samurai* warriors, transferred their loyalties from their *daimyo* (feudal lord) to the emperor, Japan was on its way toward jettisoning feudalism and becoming a modern nation-state. This second kind of Imperial Shinto overlapped with State Shinto and was outlawed after World War II. According to an official publication of the *Jinja Honcho*, the Shinto

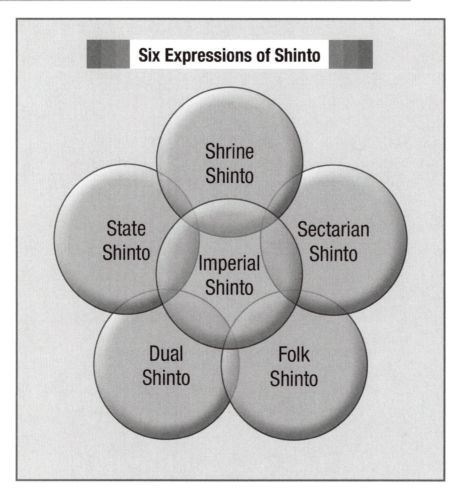

Six Expressions of Shinto

Shrine Shinto

State Shinto

Sectarian Shinto

Imperial Shinto

Dual Shinto

Folk Shinto

Shrine Association, "The Shinto of the Imperial House was the core of State Shinto, and after the denaturalization order (after World War II), it has been carried on as the rites of the Imperial House. The emperor was the center of the state in this Shintoistic sense, and at the same time was himself the high priest of the gods and the superintendent of worship of the gods."[26]

(2) **State Shinto** (*Kokka Shinto*) was once called "the national faith of Japan."[27] It arose from religious as well as political motives. In Japan, religion and politics were never far apart.

During the feudal period (C.E. 1185–1868) *shoguns,* who were military rulers of a unified Japan, had forced Shinto to merge with Buddhism; strengthening Buddhism and almost destroying Shinto. Some leaders longed for a "pure" Shinto, not the Dual Shinto that was subordinate to Buddhism. When the United States precipitated an end to Japan's feudal system with the arrival of Commodore Matthew Perry in 1853, Japan's social structures changed. Promoters of Shinto seized the opportunity to overthrow the shogunate and restore the emperor as symbolic ruler. Shinto became the state religion (April 25, 1869) but was eventually redefined as the national faith—purely Japanese patriotism. Quite soon this national faith became mixed with military aspirations. State Shinto became synonymous with militarism, imperialism, ultranationalism—and finally the atrocities of the imperial era. The Shinto Directive of 1946 outlawed State Shinto.

(3) Shrine Shinto (*Jinja Shinto*) goes back before the beginnings of Japanese written history. Shrines were already in existence at that early date. Japan's two oldest shrines, Ise Grand Shrine and Tsubaki Grand Shrine, claim to be just over two thousand years old. Beyond a doubt, Shinto shrines have existed for at least fifteen hundred years. However, there has been much development over time.

At first shrines were open-air places of worship. Even now, the idea of a dwelling or palace for kami does not quite fit with the first phase of kami worship: the calling down of the kami to receive worship, offerings, and praise. The shrine does not actually house the kami but symbols of the kami—the goshintai. At the end of the ritual, the kami are thought to return to their origin. The fact that all of this remains vague is connected to the fact that speculation is not encouraged in Shinto. Shinto is very pragmatic and prefers to focus on effective ritual and simple religious experiences rather than conjecture about mystery and the unseen.

While Shrine Shinto was co-opted by State Shinto in the decades before World War II, it has survived and reorganized itself as the Jinja Honcho, the Shinto Shrine Association. There are approximately eighty thousand shrines in the Jinja Honcho today.

Today, Shrine Shinto refers to these eighty thousand shrines that are served by at least one priest. (There are at least another one hundred twenty thousand shrines not served by priests— along roadsides, in forests, or on mountaintops.) There are several factors that determine the importance and influence of each of the eighty thousand shrines: the forty most important shrines form a hierarchy connected to the Imperial Family. A second hierarchy consists of the several hundred most famous shrines. The most important shrine or shrines in a region or province constitute a third hierarchy. (We will look more closely at shrines in the chapters on sacred time and on sacred space.)

(4) Sectarian Shinto (*Kyôha Shinto*) is the historical name of what could also be called Religious Shinto. Sectarian Shinto includes the thirteen groups[28] (or sects as they were called a century ago) that could not be merged into State Shinto—since it defined itself as pure patriotism and they were purely religious. These groups resisted becoming a part of a "national faith" movement for many reasons. One reason shared by most groups was the belief that they were chosen to purify Shinto and the Japanese people. They felt chosen to restore pure worship of the kami by ethical reform—a faith and practice that involved ethical purity as well as ritual purity. Were these groups to be included in State Shinto, there would be no way for the Japanese state to argue that Shinto was only Japanese patriotism and applied equally to all Japanese. So Sectarian Shinto was classified as a religion (*shukyo*) with other religions like Buddhism and Christianity. After the end of World War II, these groups remained separate from Shrine Shinto.

(5) Shamanic Shinto (*Minkan Shinko*[29]) is an extremely complex area of study that deals with shamans and shamanesses; spirit phenomena, including possession; and faith healing. While fraud, showmanship, and mental illness undoubtedly exist, most Shamanic Shinto accurately reflects the oldest strain of indigenous Japanese religion. Its origins extend back to a time before kami were enshrined in buildings and priests were trained in prescribed rituals. In fact, Japanese shamans received no formal training. They were either apprenticed or developed their abilities naturally through ordeals or life experience.[30]

(6) Dual Shinto (*Ryôbu Shinto*) is used to distinguish two different kinds of Shinto. One kind of Dual Shinto is called Ryôbu Shinto. It is a combination of Buddhism and Shinto in which the Buddhas were identified with the kami. This melding of religious traditions was encouraged by the Tokugawa Shogunate (1600–1867) and became almost indistinguishable from Buddhism. It was absorbed into a kind of conglomerate Buddhism. Ryôbu Shinto may have been good for the state, but it was not good for either religious tradition.

The second kind of Dual Shinto was in the realm of ideas. Since Shinto traditionally discouraged speculation, some Japanese thinkers and religionists attempted to meld psychological or philosophical thought from other systems with Shinto, in order to construct more adequate answers about meaning and purpose in life. In addition to Buddhism (especially esoteric and Tantric forms), Shinto was joined with Confucianism (for ethics and educational theory), Daoism (both mystical and devotional), and finally even Christianity (resulting in a peculiar form of millennialism and even monotheism).

Most surveys of Japan cover the "merging" of Shinto with the mainland religions of Buddhism, Daoism, and Confucianism. The merger of Buddhism and Shinto is often called **Philosophical Shinto** (each school having its own name). While this merger was mainly about ideas, there was also a merger of esoteric practices in the blending of Buddhism (Shingon and Tendai) with Shinto. Some have labeled this **Esoteric Shinto**. Finally, some authors use the term "Dual Shinto" to interpret the merger of Shinto with mountain sects, purification sects, or faith-healing sects (which some scholars see as pre-Shinto or as Buddhist).

(7) **Domestic or Family Shinto** (*Tsûzoku Shinto*) is not a category of the same order as the previous six. For this reason Domestic Shinto is not included in the graphic of the six expressions of Shinto. Domestic Shinto refers to an almost invisible form of Shinto practiced in the home without priests or public shrines. It is principally the worship of the kami in the home at the *kamidana* ("god-shelf"), a home shrine. (Some scholars use the English term Folk Shinto to be the equivalent of Domestic Shinto. If one does this, then Folk Shinto and Shamanic Shinto must be separated.)

LOOKING AHEAD

The central organizing experience of Shinto is kami, or that which is sacred. The kami experience will be our organizing principle as well. Successive chapters will approach Shinto as sacred sound, sacred story, sacred action, sacred space, sacred time, and sacred ruler. The final chapter focuses on Shinto today.

Sacred Sound

…With all the respect from the depth of our hearts
We ask that they hear us, such as the spirit
that hears our intent, with sharpened ears,
together with Spirits of the Sky and the Land,
Take the badnesses, disasters and sins and purify all.

—Amatsu Norito

SACRED LANGUAGE

It is almost impossible to step back in time into an *oral* culture of sacred word and sound. We expect every religion to have a "bible," a canon of scriptures, written down to be studied as well as used in worship. So how is it possible to project ourselves back into a time when the sounds of sacred words were so rich and powerful that they possessed the authority to convey holiness? Even today, Shinto has no revealed scripture, no writings that were dictated by a supreme being or by many beings.[31] It does, however, have sacred words that are spoken, chanted, and sung.[32] We will begin here, with words the early and even modern Japanese find sacred in the context of Shinto.[33]

It is not self-evident to non-Japanese that *the* divine language of the planet is Japanese. But that is the assumption of Shinto. (This is not unusual for tribal and ethnic religions[34]—their gods almost always speak the tribe's language. There are notable exceptions, as among shamans who journey to the land of the gods and find an unknown language or no spoken language at all—and yet understand it.) What makes it difficult for those who do not speak Japanese is that there is a widespread belief in Japan that Shinto cannot be understood—and certainly not experienced directly as it is believed that it must be—except through the medium of Japanese. This may be written off as tribal parochialism, but there is a more serious claim, namely, that there are sacred sounds (*yamato-kotoba*) that are pleasing to the divine (kami), and these sounds set in motion the possibility of divine-human contact. These sacred sounds are best located in *norito*, prayers or chants to kami in the most ancient and pure form of the Japanese language. In fact, norito are so ancient that most modern Japanese do not understand them well. Imagine hearing two-thousand-year-old English being chanted in a religious ceremony (which is impossible because English did not exist that long ago).[35]

Now imagine that you are hearing the "Great Words of Purification" (O-*Harai no Kotoba*) chanted in the morning ritual, as it is in shrines all over Japan. A few moments into the morning ritual chant you hear:

> **Koto yosashi matsuriki**
> **Kaku yosashi matsurishi kunuchi ni**
> **Araburu kamitachi o ba**
> **Kamu towashi ni towashi tamai**
> **Kamu harahi ni harahi tamaite**

Which loosely translates to:

> Profound matters were entrusted to this great kami
> [the Heavenly grandchild Sumemima no Mikoto];
> These matters of trust were to be obeyed throughout the land.
> The ways of rough malevolent kami sometimes disrupted the
> natural way of harmony.
> The great kami returned these *araburu kamitachi* [rough
> kami] to the correct path;
> They swept away all obstacles and impurities and purified the
> Ancient Land.[36]

As well as it has been translated, the English version cannot compare with the original chanted version. The words and ideas probably seem so foreign even in English that one is justified to wonder how they can be seen as sacred (even if one could construct the context from which they are taken).

The question is not whether one must be Japanese in order to practice Shinto. Some non-Japanese already practice Shinto and there are actually non-Japanese Shinto priests; for example, the Rev. Koi Barrish of Kannagara Shrine, Granite Falls, Washington, and Rev. Ann Evans of Canada. Rather, the question is: Can Shinto rituals and prayers be practiced in any language other than Japanese? That is the subject of this chapter—the nature of *kotodama*, the spiritual power residing in ancient Japanese words.

We are going to start with sacred words because they are said to invite the kami, the divinities, to come to earth or to visit a ritual and, when intoned, to send them back at the end of the ritual to wherever they have come from. These words have kami-ness, for they call the kami to a place that becomes sacred with kami presence, and the sacred words themselves create the ritual or sacred action that the worshiper participates in to experience the sacred.

Some say the words have special powers, that they are magical. They say that if the sacred words are properly pronounced and correctly used, the results are certain. This might remind some Catholics of one interpretation of the ritual of the Mass. Others may be less sure about any special magic in the words, but they know that the rituals must be done properly for the kami to be pleased and encouraged to bless the worshiper. So the sacred words appear in the invocations (*keihitsu*), prayers (norito), and imperial blessings (*yogoto*)—all must be filled with proper form and pronunciation (yamato-kotoba), and with the divine power (kotodama) of proper ritual chanting.

It may seem that these ideas would only apply to Shamanic Shinto. Yet all forms of Shinto solemnize the sacred orally. Shamanic Shinto was once free to be spontaneous in its prayers to the kami—the divine powers experienced in sacred trees, rocks, waterfalls, mountains, or coming down from the High Plain of Heaven. But now in Shrine Shinto, the norito must be learned carefully and even when new prayers are written, old forms that contain kotodama (sacred word power) must be used.

In the modern Shinto seminary, priests begin by studying the oral traditions of Shinto, *kataribe*. Kataribe literally means the "narrators"—the sacred words in story. The stories were the foundation for the Japanese classics, the *Kojiki* and the *Nihonshoki* (or *Nihonji*). The *Kojiki*'s collection of the early stories was memorized and retold by a kataribe named Hieda no Are. This oral recitation was then transcribed in a phonetic writing system that seems to have been invented just for that purpose. It chose Chinese characters only for their sound-value and wrote each Japanese syllable with a Chinese character. This seems to have been the first and last use of this awkward writing system. When the next Japanese Classic, the *Nihonshoki*, was transcribed, the scribes used pure Chinese characters.

What they lost were the sacred Japanese sounds. Yet those could *not* be lost if the narrative and the liturgy were to retain their sacred quality. Consequently, it became necessary to have two readings of each Chinese character. Thus, the Sino-Japanese reading is of *shin*, while its Japanese intonation was preserved as kami. Even though the *Nihonshoki* was written in Chinese characters, priests preserved the pronunciation (yamato-kotoba) and divine power (kotodama) of the sacred words by not abandoning the oral tradition.

THE NOTION OF SACREDNESS

Sacredness or holiness has become a central concept in the study of every religion since Rudolf Otto's famous study, *The Idea of the Holy*. It is difficult at first to grasp someone else's notion of the sacred or holy. In ancient traditions such as Shinto, some of the objects associated with the holy seem very primitive. Just how can a particular rock or a tree be sacred? But then someone who practices Shinto might ask the same of a Christian cross or a book.

Learning to observe what "presents" itself as sacred in another tradition is the first skill of a scholar of religion. Recognizing that this sacred object is not a god or an idol, but a symbol or a sign of the holiness that it points toward, is equally critical.

In this section on sacred words, some concepts seem familiar, and this invites comparisons. Comparing must be done with caution, however, or all we will do is use Shinto to repeat what we know or what we like and dislike. But when we do our homework we can discover "universals"—things common to several religious traditions.

There are also some things that are slightly shocking. For instance, so many religions believe that their own language and its sounds are the very language of the sacred or holy—worship, prayer, praise, and even discussions of truth can only occur in that one particular language. One Shinto scholar thought that Japanese had the fifty pure sounds of the universe, making it unique and the only language that was adequate to express the truths of life itself! Often such claims arise from metaphors that point in opposite directions. If taken literally, they point to exclusive truth claims. If taken symbolically, they point beyond the literal and sectarian to something that is transcendent or other than the ordinary.

SIX SACRED WORDS

Five Japanese words in addition to kami will be used to illustrate why some think that one cannot speak faithfully about Shinto in any language but Japanese. While I disagree with this assertion, there are many things to be learned by studying how Shinto is encoded in the Japanese language.

I have selected the following six words: kami, *kannagara, ki,* harai, *wa*, and *tennô*.[37] *Many* others could have been chosen. The table at the bottom of the page provides a preliminary translation and points to an issue or set of issues that is more global—a specific context or an issue in Shinto experience, practice, or ritual.

Primary Notions of Shinto
Kami (divinity)[38]

Let me begin with a conclusion: There are two seemingly conflicting meanings (usages) for the word kami. The first is as a noun that can be roughly translated as "divine beings" or

WORD	MEANING
Kami	divinity, divine, sacred, holy (issues of theism, polytheism, animism)
Kannagara	holiness and wholeness of nature (issue of animism and pantheism)
Ki	awesome power of kami-ness (issue of what is reality)
Harai	purity, purification (issue of effective salvation, attainment, or enlightenment)
Wa	harmony or peacefulness of nature (issue of person-hood and social order)
Tennô	sacredness concentrated in the person of the ruler or emperor (issue of divine or sacred rule)

"gods"; the second seems to be free of any use as a noun and functions as an adjective. It points to a quality (divine, sacred, holy) that modifies some*thing*. One meaning would lead to projecting a human shape on the kami (anthropomorphism) and would suggest a pantheon of gods in the heavens. The other meaning looked for signs of the sacred and found them almost everywhere in nature—not as heavenly beings but as powers or forces. These two tendencies may make Shinto's most important concept vague and confusing—or dynamic and mysterious.

Kami is the *kun* reading (oral Japanese) of the Chinese character that is pronounced *shin* in Japan (*shen* in Mandarin Chinese). Before looking at the experiential dimensions of kami, let us look at the comparative and linguistic problem encountered when Chinese was first used to describe Japanese religious phenomena. Kami or shin was a pejorative term as far as mainland scholars were concerned. Mainland scholars who first wrote about Japanese religion two millennia ago selected this Chinese character for the native deities of Japan (the gods or spirits) when they composed the *Nihonshoki*. (We will learn more about this book in the next chapter.) Yet, there seems to be some differences between the Chinese notion of shen (gods, deities, spirits) and the Japanese notions they sought to describe. This is an early example of the comparative study of religion facing multiple problems of translation: from one language to another (China having had a writing system for a millennia and Japan being preliterate at the time), from one religion to another (Chinese and Korean scholars using their own more devotional and ritualistic religions that were called *Shen Dao* or religious Daoism—"way of the gods"—as a basis for comparison),[39] and from one type of religion to another (polytheism in China and Korea compared to animism in Japan). But it was even more complex than the previous statement might lead one to believe. There had already been a period of "state shamanism" in which a royal priestess or shamaness, Queen Himiko, had served both as the ruler of the state and as a medium who either spoke with or was possessed by the kami. An ancient Chinese text (which long predated the *Kojiki*) talked about Japan being ruled by Himiko (or Pimiko). It was called the Queenly Kingdom, because it was ruled by a shamaness. Just how accurate these mainland descriptions were is hard to say. However, the team of scholars who completed the *Kojiki* and *Nihonshoki* were very influential in determining how the term kami would thenceforth be used.

What makes this early anthropomorphic category (shen, Chinese) so appealing is its simplicity—and that it almost got it right.[40] But it didn't—certainly not for the part of the Shinto tradition that resisted anthropomorphism. It seems that Shinto perceived the situation in exactly the opposite direction—that humans and everything else might have had something kami-like in them. But was that understanding of kami animistic?

Let's begin carefully. When data about Shinto began to be recorded in the *Kojiki*, specialists in the sacred (let's call them Shinto shamans and shamanesses for now) had already developed a view of the world that tried to account for special power and beauty, which could be found concentrated in every species—rocks, plants, animals, and humans. The most obvious thing was power or ki. We'll discuss ki in a moment, but for now let's just remember that the shamanic understanding of kami focused on experiencing kami as powerful or beautiful rather than as person or being. This notion of kami points to experience rather than belief.

Experiencing kami would require special shamanic practices or disciplines to improve sight or hearing. These practices involved privations such as long vigils without sleep, going without food and water for long periods of time, strict diets, and possibly even use of plants to alter consciousness.[41] Shamans in ancient Japan came to experience kami directly in everything. These kinds of practices tend to be lost when worship evolves into more institutional forms. It can even be argued that shamanic religion has a source of power and inspiration (the kami) that competes with earthly power, the evolving forms of government.

By the time conquerors and tyrants began to think of themselves as absolute rulers, they feared the more volatile and unpredictable shamans (and their counterparts, the prophets, who were often shamans as well). Yet both usages of the sacred word kami (as deities and as qualities) survived.

One of the best descriptions of kami is found in the scholarship of Norinaga Motoori (1730–1801) in his book, *Kojiki-den*. He was one of the persons who influenced a Shinto revival and the restoration of Imperial government in the nineteenth century. Motoori wrote:[42]

> I do not yet well understand the meaning of the word kami (and all the old explanations are wrong), but in general, the word kami refers to, first of all, the various kami of heaven and earth spoken of in the classics, and the spirits (*mitama*) enshrined in their shrines, and it goes without saying that it also refers to people, and even birds and beasts and grass and trees, ocean and mountains—and anything else that has superior and extraordinary power, provoking awe. Here, "superb" means not only superior in nobility and goodness, but also awe-inspiring things of great evil and weirdness, anything that provokes a high degree of wonder.
>
> Of people, those called kami of course include the most exalted lineage of emperors, who are called "distant kami" since they are so far removed from the ordinary person, and worthy of reverence. Then there are the human kami, who existed long ago and also at present; a certain number of human kami exist in each province, village, and house, each in accord with his or her station.
>
> The kami of the age of kami (*jindai*) were also mostly men of that time, and since all the people of that age were kami, it is called the "age of kami." Of those things that were not men, for example, lightning was known as a "sounding kami" (*narukami*), and the "sound of kami" (*kaminari*), so also the dragon and tree spirits, and foxes, since they were uncommonly mysterious, were called kami . . .

There were also many occasions on which mountains and oceans were called kami; this does not mean that a spirit (*mitama*) indwelling the mountain was called kami, but that the mountain itself, or the ocean itself, was kami, and this, too, because of their superbly awe-inspiring quality. In this way, kami are of manifold varieties, some noble and some base, some strong and some weak, some good and some evil, each being immediately in accord with its own mind and behavior.

Professor Motoori's description of kami and kami-ness is remarkable because there is a vague transcendence in the notion of heavenly kami with the rest of the references indicating immanence. Finally, kami is used as a quality of power and awe. Motoori's description points out what is essential to all kami— "superior and extraordinary power, provoking awe." This power is ki. Initially kami are not noted for what they do for society; they are not symbols of good and evil and how humans are to model civilization. They are first experienced as the awesome aspects of nature—both good and bad.

In conclusion, and simplifying somewhat, there were two broad usages of kami. The first dealt with kami as being or as an entity. When this usage of kami is what is being translated into Chinese, it is easy to see why Shen (divinities, gods, spirits) was chosen. Kami then is plural and encompasses the myriad of kami mentioned in the Japanese Classics, the *Kojiki* and the *Nihonshoki*. The second usage allows Shinto to claim that others (Chinese, Westerners) have not understood Shinto at all. It refers to the kami nature *within* something else—a tree, waterfall, etc. This usage turns kami into an adjective that modifies. So kami means "divine" or "sacred" or "holy." It is the manifestation of the sacred that one experiences.

This allows an interesting vagueness about kami. If it is discussed or defined too concretely or rationally, the charge can be made that one does not understand kami. How perfectly this works to bring one back to the point that Shinto is to be experienced instead of being discussed, believed in, or confessed.

Kannagara (divinely)

Kami is part of this compound character.[43] Grammatically, kannagara is an adverb modifying a verb (an action). It is translated into English in Shrine Shinto's *Basic Terms of Shinto* as: "An adverb modifying authoritative actions of a deity or deities, meaning divinely, solemnly, or sublimely."[44] This definition combines the two meanings of kami (anthropomorphic and adjectival) into a single description of divine action. When one acts "divinely" one is on the path of the kami and that is exactly what kami no michi means: the way or the path of the kami.

Kannagara also refers to the totality of kami. One priest explained kannagara in a more substantive way and referred to it as Mother Nature herself or "the great nature." Personified or not, kannagara looks to the sum total of all that is as it acts—divinely. Finding our way in nature is what Shinto is about.

Eventually kannagara evolved into a term for universal or cosmic harmony (wa). Sociologists think this development was a projection of the desire for harmony within the community. Irrespective of its origins, this meaning of kannagara gave birth to a vision of a unified or interrelated universe that is known as "the way of nature itself."

Ki (power)

It could be argued that ki is not one of the fundamental concepts of Shinto as it does not appear in the *Basic Terms of Shinto* published by Kokugakuin University, the premier Shinto University. I include it on the basis of a conversation I once had with the Rev. Yukitaka Yamamoto, chief priest of Tsubaki Grand Shrine. Yamamoto asked what discipline I was learning from a Shinto shamanic healer. I answered *sei-ki*.[45] He then did a beautiful calligraphy of *kami-ki* and explained why the notion of "divine energy" is one of the fundamental concepts of Shinto.

When the first mainland translators looked for a Chinese word for this power that occurs in kami, shamans, and shamannesses, they chose *qi* (breath, energy, power).[46] The Chinese court scribes despised shamans, whom they considered to be vendors of superstition. They also distrusted anything that might be a threat to the court. However, Chinese healers, herbalists, acupuncturists, and martial artists knew about qi and had developed vast literatures on the subject. For example, Chinese medicine understood qi as "vitality" or the power of the body that regulates its organs or functions.

Thus, ki means power or force, and as such it defines kami-nature or the quality of being kami. But ki was more. It was the extraordinary in anything. It could be seen or experienced directly—if not by everyone at least by the specialist, the shaman and later the priest, who could point it out and possibly enshrine it. In the *O Harai no Kotoba*, the Great Purification Ceremony, the early shamans and shamanesses called the kami to the place of worship. Another ritual, the Gishiki ceremony, sought the renewal of life power (ki). It was done for physical healing and spiritual renewal. Some rituals used the power of prayers or chants (norito) to dispel misfortune with their mysterious power (ki) that resonated with the power (ki) of kami. A ritual was worthless if it had no kami-ki.

Harai (purity)

We already encountered the sacred word harai or harae as "purification" in the "Great Purification Ceremony." One must purify oneself before worshipping the kami because they are pure. This is an important quality of kami-ness. (We will learn much more about the rituals of purification in the next chapter on sacred action.) As a sacred sound of both praise and prepa-ration, harai is the opposite of *tsumi*, meaning pollution. In the *Kogiki* and the *Nihonshoki*, the concept of pollution is physical. However, Shinto subsequently developed notions of psycholog-ical and spiritual pollution that became far more important than the idea of physical pollution. Yet the act of physically removing pollution continued to define the behavior of those who practiced Shinto, largely because it was considered to be a characteristic of the kami themselves. It can be argued that the most powerful ritual of purification is misogi, which involves standing under a waterfall. Misogi is performed in imitation of a kami who, according to a well-known story, removed the pollution of death by washing in a river. Thus, river, lake, ocean, and waterfall misogi came to symbolize the spiritual dimension of Shinto. Purity and purification are characteristics both of the kami and of the worshiper.

Wa (Harmony)

Another central notion in Shinto is that of harmony (wa, heiwa, or shôwa). The principle of harmony is central to how communal identity and ethics function in Shinto. One finds one's person-hood by harmonizing with the community through proper living, which is defined as adhering to one's role in society and fulfilling the associated responsibilities. A society or community experiences harmony when each person assumes his or her right-ful place within the whole. Attaining harmony is a continual process both among the kami (as shown by their quarrels and struggles in the Japanese Classics), and also among humans. That is why government and religion go hand in hand in Shinto. There is a divine way, and it includes the harmony that is provided by the kami.

Tennô (Heavenly Ruler)

This notion has been questioned recently but it was one of the sacred words of Shinto since the time of its first consolidation in the sixth century. The myth that describes how the head kami, the Sun Goddess Amaterasu, chose her descendant to rule the earth, provided a notion of divine rule that was always available in Shinto, even during times when it seemed to have less importance.

The idea of rule by a divine, priestly emperor connected the kami to a specific place (Japan) and its government. Even when the aristocracy or military took over the actual rule of Japan, the divine emperor's office was maintained. No matter how weak the emperor was in fact, a belief in the sacred nature of the office enabled it to survive for more than fifteen centuries.

Tennô, the emperor, was the one who brought worship (*sai*) and government (*sei*) together. The earliest Japanese term for government was *matsurigoto* (literally, "festival administration"). *Saisei itchi* is the unity (*itchi*) of worship (*sai*) and government (*sei*). After the restoration of imperial rule in the nineteenth century, one of the most important phrases was "*Sonnô*" (revere the emperor). The emperor was called "*Akitsu mi kami*" (divine emperor) and even his person was revered as "*Arahitogami*" (kami in human form).[47] The imperial system was revered as "Tennô seidô." While *Ten* (heaven) is a foreign (Chinese) concept, it was used in Japan to refer to the sacred ancestry of the emperor and his divine rule.

This concludes our discussion of sacred sound. In the next chapter we will consider sacred story as found in the narrations and in the Japanese Classics.

3

Sacred Story

. . . when the world began to be created . . .
a certain thing was produced between Heaven and Earth.
It was in form like a reed-shoot.
Now this became transformed into a God,
and was called Kuni-toko-tachi no Mikoto.

—*Nihonshoki*, Book I

SHINTO MYTHOLOGY

There is a subtle nuance to the terms "mythology" and "mythological." It implies something "nonhistorical" or "untrue." Not surprisingly, people seldom use these words with respect to their own faith. Is it fair, then, to use them to characterize someone else's faith?

Academicians use the terms "mythology" and "mythological" to designate a nonhistorical form of storytelling. Even Japanese scholars speak of Shinto as a mythological religion. Nonetheless, the terms may still be belittling. They imply that Shinto is primitive and lacking in some essentials that more advanced religions like Buddhism and Christianity might have. With this caveat in mind, let us turn to the myths of Shinto, its "sacred story," and see what depths of meaning we can find there.[48]

INDO-EUROPEAN MODEL FOR MYTHOLOGY

In my study of Hindu mythology, I arranged the subject with a set of categories and questions that worked well with Indo-European mythology.[49] Let me present those categories and questions and ask if these will work without much alteration with Shinto mythology.

The following set of questions contains certain expectations that a "good and adequate" mythology might be expected to meet. Shinto answers few of these questions adequately and its themes do not fit well into these categories. However, an additional observation needs to be made. These categories arose from the study of Indo-European mythologies. Applying them to a mythology that lies outside that family of myths for anything more than comparative purposes privileges one mythology over others. As we have already seen, privileging does not lead to real understanding. Thus, it is wrong to jump to conclusions about the superiority of one mythology over another.[50] Yet it is helpful to compare mythologies in order to see what is missing from Shinto myths. It remains for the future to have studies with appropriate categories and questions formulated from the materials of Shinto.[51]

SUBJECT	QUESTIONS
COSMOGONY, THEOGONY, ANTHROPOGONY IN GENERAL	How did the cosmos, the gods, and humans come into being? Which came first—gods or humans?
COSMOLOGY	What is the nature of the cosmos? What are the various realms or regions of the cosmos? Are there separate realms for the gods and the demons?
THEOGONY AND THEOLOGY	Where did the gods come from? What is their nature? Who are they? Are they like us in form and character? What is our relationship to them? What do they want from us?
THEOMACHY	What kept creation from being perfect? Against whom do the gods fight? Who are the demons or the demonic forces? Where did they come from? Why do they seek to destabilize the divine order that the gods created? How do they get their power? Will there ever be a final victory over evil and disorder?
ANTHROPOGONY	Where did we come from? Were humans always like this? How are we supposed to live? What are the correct traditions? What are the laws we should live by?
SOTERIOLOGY	Is there a salvation history? What must one do to be saved? Is salvation personal or in community? Is there a community that was chosen to mediate salvation?
ESCHATOLOGY	What happens at the end of time and history? Is there an afterlife? What is its nature? Can one be saved to eternal life?

From within Shinto there has been an interesting reaction to foreign judgments. Shinto has immunized itself from Western criticism with a twofold strategy: (1) translate as little as possible of the sacred treasures of Shinto from the Japanese language, and (2) maintain that only Japanese can understand and fully appreciate Shinto. Today, however, even the Jinja Honcho, the

MYTH, HISTORY, AND IDEOLOGY

The word "myth" when used by a historian of religions does not mean "fable" or "lie." Mircea Eliade's classic work on mythology describes myths as sacred stories. Eliade pointed to the deeper structures of myths, where truths could be discovered in symbolic form. Myths follow universal patterns. There are cross-cultural formats for discussing origins, sacred space, divine interventions, covenants and responsibilities, group identity, and so forth.

If taken literally, myths may justify warrior cultures and quite brutal behavior toward outsiders. But most sages in the various religious traditions teach the symbolic nature of myths. Symbols point beyond the ordinary, familiar, and local to something greater and more universal. Myths and art were the first intellectual tools used to civilize and humanize humankind—at least to the extent that we can claim humankind has been humanized at all.

History is a different kind of narrative; it asks what happened. Laying out the bare facts can be very dry, however, so historical facts are selected and arranged into meaningful stories. If there are any lessons to be learned from history, they are to be found in these selections and arrangements.

Ideology is found everywhere. At it simplest level it can be quite harmless—simply a point of view that guides the telling of meaningful stories. Ideology is dangerous when it is used to deceive. When history is falsified either by improper selection or pure lie, or when history (facts about what happened) and myth (symbolic truths) are mixed together to deceive and control, then ideology becomes a weapon to be used against outsiders. Totalitarian, militaristic and/or chauvinistic societies typically use such a deceptive ideology. Honest dialogue with persons of other views, combined with careful study of myth, history, and ideologies, can help overcome prejudice, lack of understanding, and ignorance.

Association of Shrine Shinto—Shinto's conservative umbrella organization—has begun to show interest in interfaith dialog and cooperation. This may lead to more translations of materials like the ones mentioned in this chapter.

LOOKING FOR SACRED SHINTO STORIES

Thematically, myths usually contrast order and chaos; life's duty with sin or error; responsibility with blame and culpability; knowledge and ignorance, mercy and grace with brutality, pollution, and purification; mortality and immortality; birth and fertility; asceticism and enjoyment; piety and ritualism; and demons and gods. The stories weave a tapestry that encompasses life; it becomes a worldview.

Where can we find Shinto's sacred stories? Deciding how to answer that question poses a conundrum. We would initially suppose that Shinto myths (sacred stories) are to be found in the Japanese Classics, the *Kojiki* and the *Nihonshoki*. But after learning what these books actually contain, people generally draw one of two conclusions. The older (colonial-style) conclusion complains that the Shinto myths found in the Classics are primitive, rudimentary, and incomplete. They are barely "sacred stories" at all; in fact, they are almost entirely political. The other conclusion finds the stories to have so little religious or mythological content that the collections are seen as political—or merely just folklore (however that might be defined). So we would be left with two disappointing conclusions, each leading to the understanding that Shinto's "sacred stories" can be expected to contribute little to what "sacred stories" attempt: to give deepened insights into our common human problems, our failures, and our possible aspirations.

The careful reader will guess that this assessment of Shinto's "sacred stories" is about to be questioned and that is correct. There will be several lines of argument and discovery: (1) that the Japanese Classics are a political attempt to unify some elements into a state ideology while leaving out large portions of "Shinto," (2) that Shinto's "sacred stories" lie in the materials of the cumulative tradition, that is, in both oral and written materials that we will simply call the other Shinto sources, and (3) that the "sacred stories" in the other sources have only begun to be appreciated and collected. These three lines of discovery chart the course of the remainder of this chapter.

THE JAPANESE CLASSICS

In the seventh century, Japan's Yamato clan set out to unify Shinto. This task was accomplished by leaving out large portions of indigenous and folk religion. The Yamato were not the first rulers of Japan. Chinese records indicate that a Yamatai kingdom, which they called Wa, ruled before the Yamato. However, many kingdoms existed before them, and however many regions or island principalities Japan had been divided into, the Yamato clan set out to establish themselves as the divine rulers of the first unified Japan (Nihon) since the beginning of civilized life on earth.

Until the seventh century, all Japanese sacred stories were oral—more importantly, local. There were no national stories—and no national identity. Only by order of the early Yamato royal court were these stories collected and written down. They were first collected and memorized orally, and later committed to a system of writing that used Chinese characters to represent Japanese sounds.

The task of creating collections that would serve the interests of the Yamato "imperial line" was a difficult one. It took a full half-century before, first, the *Kojiki* (712), and then the *Nihonshoki* (720), were presented to the court. Ironically, by the time these collections were ready, the imperial court had changed its mind. Instead of adopting Shinto as the state religion, the court turned to esoteric Buddhism and specifically to the idea that the ruler was an incarnation of a *boddhisattva* (a Buddha-to-be). It was Buddhist mythology—not Shinto mythology—that buttressed the Yamato claim to divine selection to run the emerging empire. Even before the imperial capitol was founded in Nara (710), the Yamato court proclaimed

Buddhism to be the state religion (594). Shinto would serve as a mere handmaiden of that decision. Those who collected Shinto's "sacred stories" in such a way as to portray the Yamato ruler as the divine descendant of the Sun Goddess (Amaterasu Ômikami) failed in their initial attempt to convince the court that Shinto should be the state religion.

Shinto was given its own imperial office at court and regulated. "Shinto" was the collective term used for those who worshipped the kami. This distinguished Shinto from Buddhism, Confucianism, Daoism, and various Chinese religio-philosophical schools such as the *yin-yang* and the five-elements traditions. Some of the vast Japanese indigenous tradition was legitimated and the rest (whatever the court did not want and did not find useful) was proscribed. The shrine tradition was encouraged and assigned ranks. It was awarded generous gifts from the court and honors. Shrines were even given fiefs. Of course each of these actions was taken in order to encourage the kind of Shinto favored by the court. The imperial influence went even further; it outlawed Shamanic or Folk Shinto. There seemed to have been little overt persecution. It was almost impossible for the Nara court to reach very far beyond central Honshu in religious matters, especially among the masses. But for those desirous of currying imperial favor, the message was clear: only certain practices would be encouraged and rewarded.

The earliest example of the imperial court's attempt to merge Buddhism and Shinto began very simply. The court asked its most loyal shrine at Ise to promote the making of a great bronze Buddha for the capitol at Nara. The chief priest of Ise Grand Shrine performed a divination and received an oracle from the kami requesting the people to give precious metals for the construction of the giant Buddha. This would indirectly grant support for the court's choice of Buddhism as the state religion. The Great Buddha was dedicated at Tôdaiji in Nara in 752.

The members of the Imperial court who favored Shinto received Shinto materials in a style that copied Chinese gazettes or *Fudoki*. These local gazettes were ordered by the imperial court in 713. The only gazette surviving more or less intact is the one from Izumo. It is important because a political reading of the *Kojiki* and *Nihonshoki* would see the region of the Izumo clan as the last real opponent to the rule of the Yamato clan. The *Izumo Fudoki* of 733 presents a different portrayal of Okuninushi-no-Mikoto (the kami of the sea reverenced at Izumo) than the one found in the Japanese Classics. In the *Kojiki* and *Nihonshoki*, Okuninushi is a descendant of the chaotic brother of the Sun Goddess, and therefore a symbol of what had to be civilized for divine order to come to earth.

The Izumo mythology put forward a strong and independent claim to divine descent. The Izumo claimed descent from Amaterasu's older brother, Susanoo-no-mikoto, who was ruler of the earth. (The imperial version made him a younger brother.) Perhaps the other regional gazettes that survived only as fragments presented similar claims. Whatever the case, eventually the Shinto party at court would abandon their project of collecting, editing, and republishing a unified Shinto mythology. Without the adoption of Shinto as the state religion, the early drive toward a unified "Shinto" religion lost momentum. Thus, Shinto did not acquire a canonical scripture, as many other religions did as part of their drive toward unity and adoption as the established religion of a state.

Unification of Shinto mythology never took place. The court seemed happy with a semiunified Shinto for more than a thousand years. Shinto was semiunified by means of several court actions. A Shinto office was established in the imperial court. Shinto shrines were ranked according to their assigned importance. The court visited important shrines and performed imperial worship there. Imperial offerings given to favored shrines constituted a large portion of the wealth of those shrines. The court granted land and even entire villages to shrines. Favored Shinto priests were awarded court appointments and honors.

I turn next to a consideration of the Japanese Classics, the *Kojiki* and the *Nihonshoki*. This will be followed by a summary of their storyline about the age of the kami.

Kojiki

This Japanese classic based on oral traditions was compiled in 712. It relates myths, legends, and historical accounts centering around the imperial court, from the age of the gods until the reign of Empress Suiko (593–628). Shinto theology has developed largely through the interpretation of *Kojiki* mythology. The ceremonies, customs, taboos, magic practices, and divination practices of ancient Japan are described in great detail.

The *Kojiki* is a remarkable document from the point of view of language. Since the Japanese were preliterate, their oral language was written down phonetically, choosing Chinese characters not for their meaning but for their sound. The *Kojiki* is most difficult to read because it requires a scholarly knowledge of written Chinese as well as an oral knowledge of the most ancient Japanese words known as yamato-kotoba (see chapter two). The *Kojiki* shows most clearly the process of selection by or for the Yamato court; a single version of the mythology is selected and it attempts, quite poorly at times, to tell a coherent story about the divine origin of the Japanese people and their imperial line.[52]

> According to the preface of the *Kojiki*, Temmu lamented that the records of the "various houses" (presumably the imperial and courtier houses) had been altered and falsified, and ordered a man at court named Hieda no Are, who possessed a fabulous memory, to memorize an imperial genealogy and a collection of ancient narratives.... The *Kojiki*, whose editing was completed in 712 by the courtier O no Yasumaro (d. 723), is a book in three parts. Part one deals with the age of the gods from the time when the first deities appeared, as heaven and earth took shape, up to the birth of the future emperor Jimmu. Part two covers the period from Jimmu through Emperor Ojin, the fifteenth sovereign in the traditional chronology; part three traces the imperial succession from Nintoku.[53]

The *Nihonshoki*

The Chronicles of Japan were presented to the court only eight years after the *Kojiki,* and its first two books corresponded roughly to the first volume of the *Kojiki.*[54] Thirty volumes of historical narratives cover the time from the age of the gods through the reign of Empress Jitô (690–697). The first half of the work contains many myths and legends, while the latter half is more historically reliable. By comparison with the *Kojiki,* the *Nihonshoki* left more of the individual myths intact. It did not filter the myths as much in order to come up with the most favorable version for the Yamato court. "While the *Kojiki* gives only one version of each of the stories that constitutes the sequence of myths in the age of the gods, the *Nihonshoki* often provides three, four, or more versions of a story, such as the birth of Amaterasu and her elevation to rulership over heaven or the descent of Ninigi to earth."[55]

Because it was written in pure Chinese, the *Nihonshoki* was easier to read than the *Kojiki.* It was also more influenced by Chinese thought and literary conventions. There has been much speculation regarding the intended purpose of the first two books of the *Nihonshoki.* They either reflect the first stage of gathering of available myths, which would ultimately be restructured into a unified mythology teaching the divine origin of the Yamato rule, or their purpose was to collect the ancient stories in all their variety and for their own sake, as is the case in modern ethnology. No ancient ruling house was secure enough to collect materials that would encourage other claimants to contest their rule, so it is most unlikely that the *Nihonshoki* was intended to be a collection of the variety of early myths in Japan. "In fact, the *Nihonshoki* became the first of six national histories (*rikkokushi*), the last of which ends with the death of Emperor Koko (884–887)."[56]

It is fascinating to observe how, in this way, small and remote Japan, even in an age when it appeared to be importing the entirety of Chinese culture and civilization, asserted its own national uniqueness and superiority. Here is the complete *bansei ikkei* myth: the concept of Japan as a land created by and therefore "of" the gods, and as a land superior to all others both because of its sacred origins and because it was to be ruled always by a single family descended from the Sun Goddess. This myth remained an unchallenged orthodoxy in Japan until the end of World War II.

> ... at different times and in different ways [they] served as the scriptures of Shinto. The first great flourishing in the study of the *Nihonshoki* occurred during the medieval age (the late twelfth through the late sixteenth centuries), when scholars devoted their attention almost exclusively to the examination of and research into the book's first section, the "age of the gods." [57]

Let's summarize what can be said at this point. First, the Japanese Classics, the *Kojiki* and the *Nihonshoki*, are not just about "sacred stories" or mythology; they are equally concerned with providing political support for the ruling family. Second, only a few of the many Shinto sacred stories were selected for inclusion in the Japanese Classics. Third, the *Kojiki* and the *Nihonshoki* have similar structures, but the *Nihonshoki* generally contains several versions of each myth while the *Kojiki* will have only one version of each myth. The fact that the *Nihonshoki* contains variants of a myth suggests that it represents a project that was not completed. Fourth, the Classics did not become sacred scripture, yet their central idea (rule by a divine descendant of the Sun Goddess) became an unquestioned belief in all later types of Shinto, as well as in later state ideology.

A SUMMARY OF THE SACRED STORY
OF THE JAPANESE CLASSICS

The age of the kami (the *Kami-yo*) is a time of beginnings. (It does not matter that Shinto priests at the same shrine and certainly at different shrines have quite different stories to tell.

The stories are imaginal—for the beauty of the language and the power of emotions.)

When heaven and earth began, three kami (*zôka-sanshin*, three primal creators) came into being (*naru*) in the High Plain of Heaven (*Takamahara*). Later kami were born (*umareru*).[58]

At least six divine generations of kami were born before two parent kami, Izanagi and Izanami, were born. The later generations of kami come in pairs—translated from the ancient terminology as brother and sister.[59] The collective kami command Izanagi and Izanami to "make, consolidate, and give birth to this drifting land."[60] They are given a jeweled spear with which they stir the brine below from the Floating Bridge of Heaven. The brine curdled, dripped from their spear and made an island, Onogoro.[61] They descend to Onogoro and build a pillar and a hall. Then they attempt to carry out their mission, but it does not come easily. They circle the pillar and unite, creating Hiruko, the leech-child.[62] She is so malformed that they send her to sea in a reed boat. They then gave birth to the island of Aha. Both of these children were considered "not good," so the divine parents ascended to heaven and reported all this to the collective kami. By divination, the august ones found out that the birth mishaps were caused by the female kami (Izanami) speaking first in the circling ritual. After this is corrected, the creations go well. Next came a long list of island births, each with exuberant names, including an island chain called "Great-Yamato-the-Luxuriant-Island-of-the-Dragon-fly" or "Land of the Eight Great Islands."[63] After these island-countries are born, they gave birth to more than thirty kami whose lavish names would not generate cults of ritual and devotion but served as symbols for the collective forces of nature on earth.[64] Then came disaster with the birth of the kami of fire, named three different ways in the *Kojiki* (Fire-Burning-Swift-Male kami, Fire-Shining-Prince kami, and Fire-Shining-Elder kami). He burns his mother so severely during childbirth that she becomes sick. This produces another kind of creation—birth from the deity's body parts, even her excrement that might otherwise seem impure.[65]

When Izanami dies, Izanagi's tears give birth to the Crying-Weeping-Female kami who dwells at Konomoto.[66] Izanagi buried his wife-sister on Mount Hiba near Izumo.[67] Then Izanagi drew his saber in anger and killed his fire-child. From the blood of the child eight kami are born, those of the august sword.

After his grief and anger subside, Izanagi decides to go into the underworld of the dead, *Yomi-no-kuni* (or just *Yomi*). He finds Izanami residing in a palace and asks her to come back and help him finish making the lands. She wanted to return with him so she went back into the palace to discuss the matter with the Yomi kami. She took so long that Izanagi made a torch from a strand of his ample hair and went inside the palace to find her. What he found were maggots, decay, and a rotting wife. Izanami felt shamed and sent the Ugly-Female-of-Yomi, then eight Thunder kami, and finally fifteen hundred warriors to punish him. That having failed, Izanami attempted to catch him herself, but Izanagi threw a great rock over the mouth of the entrance to Yomi, and there they exchanged their last words. Izanami's curse seems to be the source of human death.

Izanagi went to the Island of Tsukushi and cleansed himself in a small river; this became the model for misogi, the ritual of purification. As he throws off his garments, twelve more kami are born. He went into the middle of the river and began washing off the pollution. First the Wondrous-kami-of-Eighty-Evils (tsumi) and then Wondrous-kami-of-Great-Evils are born from the filth that he washes away. Three kami to rectify evil are followed by a number of ocean-possessing kami. These latter kami are mentioned as being associated with specific clans. Finally, Izanagi washes his left eye and Amaterasu-o-mi-kami, the Sun Goddess (Heaven-Shining-Great-August-kami), is born. When he washed his right eye the moon god, Tsuki-yomi-no-mikoto, was born, and when he washed his nose Susanoo-no-mikoto (some say a star god, others the god of storms) was born. Susanoo has the ominous literal name of Brave-Swift-Impetuous-Male-Augustness.[68] More than fifty kami have preceded Amaterasu but she will be the most important kami of the Kami-yo, the divine age. She will become the ruler of the High Plain of Heaven.

Izanagi then installed his three children—Amaterasu, Tsukyomi, and Susanoo—as rulers of heaven, night, and sea (and/or land), respectively.[69] But Susanoo's storms (made pathetic in the text as weeping) ruined the land, and Izanagi expelled him when Susanoo said that he wanted to go to be with his mother. Susanoo then went up to the High Plain of Heaven to take leave of his sister, Amaterasu, but even there he commits a sacrilege by destroying her rice fields and her silk weaving looms.[70] In fear, Amaterasu escapes into a cave, the Rock-Dwelling (*Ame-no-Iwato*), plunging the world into darkness. The heavenly kami perform a ritual using the sacred *sakaki* (evergreen) branch, along with divinations and offerings, to propitiate her, but it does not work. Then Ame-uzume-no-mikoto (the Heavenly-Alarming-Woman, Uzume) danced in such a fashion as to make all the eight myriad kami shout and laugh, bringing Amaterasu out of the cave to see how there could be laughter in spite of cosmic darkness. The kami succeed in sealing the cave so that darkness and calamity will not return. Uzume becomes the kami of dance, culture, and literature. Her most important role, however, is as a divine emissary to clear the way for the rule of Amaterasu's grandson, Ninigi-no-mikoto (or Ninigi). Uzume uses her exceeding charms to marry the giant kami of Earth, Sarutahiko Okami, who guards the roads and paths of Earth. After many adventures, the rule of Earth is finally turned over to Amaterasu's grandson, Ninigi. When the Kami-yo comes to a close, it is one of Ninigi's descendants who begins the imperial age, with Jimmu Tennô as the first emperor of Nihon ("land of the sun's origin," "land of the rising sun"), land of the kami.[71]

SOME CONCLUSIONS ABOUT THE CLASSICS

The emergent state "Shinto" of the *Kojiki* and the *Nihonshoki* was polytheistic, with Amaterasu, a rather late goddess in the order of creation (eighteenth!), finally reaching the top of a pantheon of heavenly kami—who are clearly gods and goddesses. This polytheism was constructed for one purpose: to legitimate the claim of the Yamato clan to be the eternal and divine rulers of Nihon, "the land of the rising sun" and therefore "the land of the kami."

Through a rather incomplete logic, Amaterasu's grandson, Ninigi, will begin a line of descendants who will claim rulership of the earth. The Classics do not clearly state which kami was the previous ruler of the earth. The elder (or younger) brother of Amaterasu was Susanoo, who was depicted variously as the Star God, the Storm God, or the God of the Sea. He was given rule over earth by the collective kami, but after his profane actions in heaven he became the target of his sister's attempts to replace him. Because Susanoo is an ujigami (clan deity) of the Izumo clan,[72] the Classics must prove that Susanoo and his descendants are unworthy to rule earth anymore, and that their right to rule has been ceded to Amaterasu's descendants.

The Classics inadvertently mention another kami, who is chief of the earthly kami. This is Sarutahiko, the pioneer kami and chief kami of Tsubaki Shinto. This region is already an ally of the Yamato, so any of their claims for their kami and his divine descendants have been assimilated into the storyline of the *Kojiki*, the more coherent of the two Classics.

The project of writing sacred history remained incomplete. Even as the many clan mythologies began to be collected, the Yamato, or imperial court, was discovering Chinese culture and Buddhism. The Nara court would no longer need a unified Shinto for its legitimization once it had discovered the notion of a "righteous ruler" in Buddhism. The court was especially attracted to the myth of a ruler who is a reincarnated Buddha or boddhisattva, and a manifestation of Daiinichi Buddha, the great sun Buddha.[73]

Confucianism arrived during this time of empire building, but it was not nearly as influential in Japan as it had been in imperial China and Korea, where it enjoyed a monopoly over education and ritual. Shinto adopted the Confucian designation of the emperor as the "son of heaven" (*Tianzi*, *T'ien Tzu*), but transformed it into the twofold notion of (1) the ruler's divine descent from Amaterasu, the Sun Goddess, and (2) divine selection of Japan's ruling family.

It was the Yamato, the champions of rice cultivation and silk production, who unified Japan. Some have argued that rice cultivation and silk production provided an economic basis for unification, and for conquest of the fishing and hunting cultures in the rest of Japan. The Yamato's claim that they introduced rice and silk may not have been historically accurate, but they managed to place their claim into the sacred stories.[74]

LOOKING FOR OTHER SOURCES

The *Kogoshui* (Gleanings from Ancient Stories) was produced by the court ritualists, the Imbe clan, and contains stories not found in the *Kojiki* and the *Nihonshoki*.[75] H. Paul Varley points out the significance of the fact that many of its stories deal with the history of the Imbe. When the Imbe compiled the *Kogoshui* in C.E. 807, their main purpose was to combat the ascendancy of the rival Nakatomi family in Shinto affairs at court.[76]

The gazettes, the *Fudoki*, have already been mentioned. They were collected in the eighth century and point to the existence of a larger tradition in which each important shrine had its own sacred stories about its origin and about its particular kami or clan deities (ujigami).

Manyôshû (Collection of a Myriad Leaves)

The oldest anthology of Japanese verse was compiled in the eighth century.[77] It contains 4,500 poems, the earliest of which is attributed to a fourth-century empress (placing it prior to the historical period). Most of the poems in the *Manyôshû* date from between the fifth and the eighth centuries. They were written by persons of various ranks, from emperors to peasants. The *Manyôshû* was noted for its straightforward expression of sentiment. It also provided valuable information about ancient religious beliefs, customs, mores, and thought. Though not on a par with the *Kojiki* and the *Nihonshoki*, the *Manyôshû* does contain elements of Shinto mythology that help to fill in the puzzle of Shinto origins. Worship or reverence of ancestors was not mentioned, while thirty-six mountain kami and twenty-two sea kami are named.[78]

The *Enjishiki* (begun in 905) is the oldest surviving collection of early imperial regulations and penal codes. Of its fifty volumes, the first ten are related to Shinto. They contain some of the oldest known prayers (norito). An imperial code known as the *Jingiryô* contained laws concerning the kami and prescribed how imperial coronations were to be done. The *Jingiryô* also included regulations regarding the major annual festivals (*matsuri*).

There are later written resources that must be noted, not for the sake of the state ideology of divine descent, but for the larger worldview of Shinto. Five books collectively known as the *Shinto Gobusho* are assigned by scholars to the thirteenth century. They present the main teachings of Ise Shinto[79] and reflect a harmonizing or unifying movement with Ise Grand Shrine as the central shrine of Shinto. Because examinations and promotions[80] were and are based on them, these books have attained a quasi-scriptural status. They have been called the "Shinto Pentateuch" (the nickname comes from the first five books of the Jewish Bible/Christian Old Testament).

Shinto resources like the *Shinto Gobusho* have not been translated into other languages because (1) it is believed that such treasures can only be understood in the Japanese language (see chapter two) and (2) it is believed that these treasures cannot be understood by foreigners even in translation. Such attitudes are changing as evidenced by the work of Chief Priest Yamamoto of Tsubaki Grand Shrine, about whom more will be said in the final chapter.

When all is said and done, Shinto was represented by a vast amount of written and oral source material. Shinto's many resources functioned in place of a scripture or an authoritative canon. When Shinto was the state religion, the Japanese Classics functioned as scripture. Features that emphasized divine rule of a divine empire worked well during that period. When Shinto was not the state religion an opposing, pluralistic tradition came to the fore, allowing thousands of individual shrines and their sacred stories to flourish.

A POSTSCRIPT

The recovery of the sacred stories of the entire Shinto tradition will require a great deal of future research. Under State Shinto, forced unification narrowed the many narratives into the state ideology. After the Shinto Directive of 1946, Shinto was free to recover its many sacred stories, but unification remains a central concern of the Shrine Association (Jinja Honcho). Sadly, much of the diversity has already been lost.

4

Sacred Action

*... the Heavenly gods will
push open Heaven's eternal gates,
and cleaving a path with might
through the manifold clouds of Heaven,
will hear ... and the mists of the low hills, will bear.*

—Purification Ritual, The Yengishiki

When we looked—following good Western precedents for studying religion—in Shinto's oldest books to find the heart of its faith and practice, we discovered that not only does Shinto have no divinely revealed scripture, but, in addition, its oldest books do not contain its complete view of the world. Now we turn our attention to the encoded worldview of Shinto's rituals and ceremonies.

Rituals and ceremonies carry meaning and significance in much the same way that cultural gestures disclose the agreed-upon meanings found within that culture. Just as a handshake or a kiss can have numerous meanings depending upon context and style of expression, so too do Shinto rituals carry numerous meanings and signals for those within Japanese culture. From claps and bows to voiced sounds and performed music, coded messages surround ritual events at both conscious and pre-conscious levels. Shinto, however, has little interest in decoding the meanings of actions. This lack of interest in intellectual explanation helps to explain why it is often said that one cannot learn Shinto; one must catch it. Catching it means doing it, for Shinto is an action-centered religion.

As an action-centered religion, Shinto differs from devotional religion. It does not focus on a personal relationship with a particular deity. Rather, it centers on *doing* as the primary vehicle for experiencing the sacred, the holy, or the divine. The experience of the sacred is immediate, in the here and now, and via the senses. It comes from seeing, hearing, tasting, smelling, touching—as well as doing, dancing, acting, and engaging. Something different from the ordinary is encountered directly and one is momentarily transformed. Within the context of an action-centered religion, one cannot speak sensibly about "mere ritual," for ritual is the heart of divine activity. One is most likely to encounter the holy while engaged in shared activities. The Shinto community is dedicated to finding wholeness and unity through proper actions and behaviors. By acting properly, or, as Shinto would say, by acting purely, one comes into the realm of divine community and its power (ki) to manifest the sacred.

PARTICIPANT-OBSERVATION

I was preparing to be a participant-observer in misogi, Shinto's waterfall purification ritual. The process elicited every prejudice my Protestant, antiritualistic background could provide. Why, I asked myself, couldn't the priests articulate what we were going to do in some sensible (theological or philosophical) way? Why was I standing in a loincloth in the middle of a winter blizzard chanting ancient formulas that even my Japanese translator (who, by the way, was safely in his ski jacket) had no idea how to translate?

Shinto was the first faith tradition I had studied that provided virtually no access to its worldview through scripture, through mythology, or even through the explanations of its adherents. So I was there to see and experience whatever I could. Luckily, I found one of the only Shinto shrines in the late 1970s that would permit a foreigner to experience its most sacred rituals. That misogi experience would launch a journey of discovery that would lead, ultimately, to the recognition that Shinto ritual encodes another way of experiencing the sacred. I coined a term for this new way of experiencing the sacred, "actional religion"; relying upon the ancient fourfold model of India[81] but developing that model in a direction that made it more suitable for transcultural and interfaith applications.

Sacred sounds, sacred words, and sacred stories mingle with sacred action in the rituals of Shinto. We learned that the sacred language and the words of the gods, the divine words of the kami, did not provide doctrines. Shinto is heard in the offering of sacred words as prayers (norito), which are chanted to call the kami to receive worship, and chanted again to send the kami home at the end of the ceremony. Even that interpretation is too literal for some. It is very much in the spirit of Shinto to be vague and mysterious.

Both the sacred sounds and the sacred stories prescribe that worship should be done in a solemn and correct manner. The spontaneity of Shamanic Shinto has long since disappeared. Now a specialist, a priest or priestess, must conduct worship in prescribed ways that are formal and exact.

RITUAL AND ACTION-CENTERED
RELIGIOUS EXPERIENCE

Action-centered religion transforms persons through doing or acting. All other religious practice is subordinated to action, and one feels really alive religiously or spiritually in the here-and-now of acting, doing, practicing, and performing. If one or more of the five senses are not involved then one is not engaged in an action-centered religious experience.

Beliefs and explanations are secondary to the practices themselves. This annoys Westerners who are constantly asking: "Why is this done?" or "What does this mean?" When explanations are not forthcoming, Westerners may assume that the lack of explanation indicates (1) lack of religious—in other words, devotional—content, (2) loss of religious content, or (3) ignorance on the part of the particular informer.

In its orientation toward the sacred, Shinto must be classified as an immanent rather than a transcendent religion. Shinto finds the sacred in this very world—in nature. Transcendent religious experience, which is the opposite of immanent religious experience, posits a God who is radically different from the things of this world. Metaphorically, immanent religion is the horizontal plane of religious experience. In immanent religion, the sacred is experienced in nature, in human life, and in community. We might speak of the glory of God filling the earth, or of God dwelling in our midst. Transcendent religion, on the other hand, is the vertical plane of religious experience. Here we might speak of God as being far above and beyond us and anything that we might know. While there are religious systems that attempt to combine both immanent and transcendent religious experience, Shrine Shinto falls comfortably into the immanent category.

Ritual is the heart of action-centered religion. Ritual is not just an appendage or an artifact from the past. In action-centered religion, ritual is central. Ritual can be defined as an action or series of actions that are intentionally directed toward the sacred. ("Action" in this context includes the use of the voice for prayer, chanting, and song.) All societies and all ages have engaged in ritual behavior; finding therein a vast reservoir of life-preserving and life-enriching possibilities. Because of its focus on the here-and-now, Shinto's ritually prescribed ways of moving and behaving can provide immediate satisfaction for participants. But rituals also have long-lasting effects. Rituals encode etiquette, values, and ethics. When ethics is transmitted through ritual, there is no need to rely on a set of commandments or laws.

ATTENDING A SHINTO RITUAL

You arrive at a Shinto shrine. You join a group at the beginning of a festival commemorating the changing seasons. Upon entering the shrine, you wash your hands and mouth at a spring-fed pavilion (*temizu-ya*) with proper gestures and respect (*temizu*). An additional purification is performed by the priest as you enter the shrine. He waves a wand of paper streamers (*haraigushi*) over all the worshippers' heads. You may then make an offering of money to the kami. This can be done with two claps, a bow, and then a request.

The priests bring offerings and places them before the main shrine. Some have been prepared by the shrine, others (fruit, vegetables, sake) are brought by the worshipers. At this particular ceremony, the chief priest opens the *honden*'s doors (the holy of holies), inviting the kami to the festival. The sacred objects (goshintai) cannot be seen because of a veil but that hidden presence adds to the ceremony, creating the sensation of being seen by the kami.

A ritual prayer (norito) is read by the priest before the kami, and then an offering of evergreen branches (*tamagushi*) is made in a prescribed manner. If the group is quite large, as at a festival, then representatives receive the honor of performing the tamagushi for the community. Now you and the community proceed to an inner sanctuary and partake of a symbolic feast, which is actually a few sips of rice wine (*sake*) and sometimes a sweet. This represents eating with the kami—receiving their blessing and abundance. You are also given a specially prepared gift, including a number of objects that can be placed on your kamidana ("god-shelf").

As part of a group you may request a performance of the shrine's sacred dance (*kagura*). And you are moved by this re-enactment of ancient meanings and symbols. As you watch, you may have a sense of becoming more kami-like through the ritual.

Other elements include processions both before and after the ceremony at the main shrine. Drumming marks the call to the main shrine and the end of that ceremony. Sacred music—usually recorded but with live musicians for major festivals—is performed to please the kami as well as the worshipers. At major festivals, the shrine's own tradition of dance will be performed by the shrine maidens (*miko*). Visits to important sites within the shrine compound, either guided or simply wandering, are part of the experience of nature and beauty.

The preceding description represents an "outsider's view." Let's look at what one of the participating priests said about the same ritual.

AN INSIDER'S VIEW OF THE CEREMONY [82]

The ceremony began with *Syubatsu*, the purification of the *shinsen* (food offerings), the ceremonial objects, the priests, the participants, and the area. This was performed by the Shinto priest, the *kannushi* (meaning belonging to and dedicated to serving kami).

Another priest recited the words of purification (*Harae-Kotoba*), calling on the Kami of purification (Haraedo-no-ohkami) to cleanse the area of any impurity (*kegare*) that may obscure the pure energy of divine nature.

The *ohnusa* (officiating priest) waved the haraigushi (wand of purification and antenna for the *haraedo-no-ohkami*) to sweep away stagnation and I, as *ento* (assisting priest), sprinkled water with salt, the purifier of life.

The highest ranking or chief priest at the ritual then opened the doors of the inner sanctuary as another priest voiced the keihitsu, the awe-inspiring "oh" sound. (The doors of the inner sanctuary are opened only three times a year, at the Spring, Fall, and annual ceremonies.) This was followed by *kensen*, the offering of food (shinsen) to kami. As the *Saisyu*, or master of the ceremony, the chief priest dedicated the prayer, *norito-soujyou*. The vibration and rhythm of the norito resonates with the ki (energy) of kami by means of a special, inbred, mysterious power.

The chief priest prayed for the happiness, health, prosperity, and protection of all, and expressed gratitude to kami. Those in attendance at the ceremony appeared more keenly aware of a feeling of purification than they were of the 100-degree-plus heat.

A shrine maiden (miko) dedicated the sacred dance to kami, the *Kagura-mai Urayasu-no-mai*. The timeless dignity, grace, and beauty of this offering was felt deeply by all.

The offering of tamagushi followed kagura (sacred dance). Tamagushi is a branch of evergreen with a *shide* (paper helix) attached with *asa-himo* (hemp). The shide is an antenna sensitive to kami and the asa-himo is straight and clear as kami energy. *Tama* refers to tamashii (soul) and *gushi* to *kushi* (to connect).

Tamagushi-hairei (offering) is a profound method for personal connection to kami. Saisyu (master of the ceremony) led the kannushi in this dedication. They were followed first by honored guests and then by other guests.

Following tamagushi-hairei, the food offering was symbolically removed by covering the main offering. Then a final bow was made to kami.

The chief priest thanked guests for attending and gave a brief talk. He explained how Tsubaki America has been very active in interfaith dialogue and has provided academic opportunities for Shinto studies. He said that Shinto, which transcends the domain of religion, provides a "spiritual mechanism" to balance the modern mind. He assured everyone that Tsubaki America and its resident priest would continue to work for a deeper mutual understanding between Japan and the United States and for world peace.

Analyzing the simplest of Shinto rituals is not always successful. Many Western observers used to say that "Shinto ritual has little reverence and almost no explanation." Both of those criticisms are from the perspective of an "outsider" and therefore may not accurately reflect what is happening for the worshiper. Admittedly, such conclusions may have been reached only after experiencing the frustration of interviewing dozens of worshipers and priests and not obtaining a suitable explanation. Furthermore, if devotional religious experiences are seen as the standard, then perhaps these criticisms are somewhat justified. They do miss the point, however, which is to understand how ritual is able to spiritually transform someone.

Let's consider some of the most common objections to rituals:

(1) "The ceremony or ritual is too long." It is true that rituals can be quite long and might even repeat many elements.

(2) "It lacks intellectual sophistication." This is wrong, as we will soon see.

(3) "It is too relaxed; people are not paying attention or participating all the time." This may be true of ritualized worship all over the globe—from the Roman Catholic mass to the Hindu sacraments (*sadhyas*). It is true that Shinto priests occasionally seem to relax and not take their activity in the worship seriously, but every ritual action has a standard by which it is unconsciously measured—priests and worshipers know when an excellent ceremony has been performed. Rituals performed without a proper atmosphere of reverence do elicit the accusation that they are being done solely for money. The abuse of religious rites is a universal problem; however, Shinto is no more guilty than other religions.

(4) "The prayers are memorized or read and obviously performed 'before the kami.'" This is true, but one must understand that it is of the essence of ritual that things

should be done in this manner. Action-centered religion holds that there is a proper form for worship that must be enacted. Ritualized prayer is not a one-on-one conversation with God, as it is supposed to be in devotional religion. Action-centered religion uses a solemn and formal style of worship with exact rules for every procedure. Not informality and spontaneity, but rather formality, predictability, consistency, and reliability are characteristic of ritualized worship.

(5) "Offering the deities food and drink is primitive and even childish." This may be true if taken literally. Literalness is supposed to be outgrown in late childhood. As an adult, a worshiper is expected to find symbolic and metaphoric meanings in ritual. Ritual fails if the worshiper does not understand the symbolic use of sacred action, and does not know that sacred actions point to something other than their ordinary, everyday meaning. For example, offerings of food and drink do not mean that the kami are hungry and thirsty; they symbolize a divine-human interaction that celebrates life and its gifts.

(6) "Water, and therefore water rituals (temizu), do not remove moral impurities; nor does sweeping away of moral contaminants with the haraigushi." This criticism, like the previous one, comes from a literal perspective. Water purifications, taken literally, can remove no more than physical dirt. However, if the worshiper moves to the level of symbolic understanding, then water purification pertains to psychological and spiritual healing, renewal, and growth.

ELEMENTS OF SHINTO RITUAL

The first preparation for sacred action is water purification. There is a set of actions called temizu, cleansings of the hands and mouth. The worshiper first takes a wooden dipper in the right hand and rinses the left with fresh water. Then the right hand is rinsed. With the dipper in the right hand, water is poured into the left and that water is used to rinse the mouth. The worshiper then steps back and empties the used water onto the ground. The dipper is placed back in correct position for the next worshiper to take it. The worshiper is now ready for a further purification by a priest, this time with the sacred wand (haraigushi), which is the ritual implement used in

SACRED RITUALS AND CEREMONIES

Someone else's rituals often appear almost childish. It is equally surprising to learn that others' opinions of our rituals are often just as judgmental and ill-informed. Seeing how religious behavior is informed by the sacred is an acquired or learned skill. It happens naturally for those who grow up in a tradition. It seems so natural that even the questions of adolescence are usually transformed into adult faith; and this occurs across religions.

Action-centered religions like Shinto place rituals at the center of their experience of the sacred. They subordinate other types of religious expression to what is done (acted). Thus, rituals carry most of the burden of informing the worshipper about the sacred. The ritual must be done well, with beauty, solemnity, and grace—and regularly. If it is done poorly or superficially, the rituals will *not* convey a sense of awe and mystery about life and all its questions. Action-centered religion makes less use of deep feelings than devotional religion, and it has fewer intellectual explanations than religion centered on cognition. Both emotions and intellect can be used to make up for any deficiency in ritual experience; that is why many religions have blended rituals with devotion. At this point in time, Shinto has done relatively little of this blending. It remains almost exclusively centered on ritual.

Misogi is an example of a Shinto ritual. It is a water-purification ritual. The idea of symbolically washing away impurities and contamination is very old. If taken literally instead of symbolically, washing off moral and spiritual impurities seems a childish idea. However, doing this purification in a cold waterfall in winter can be an arresting experience. One may wake up to ways in which one is not in harmony with nature, life, one's neighbors, or one's own self. Cold water misogi can be a transforming event in one's life.

harae. Linen or paper streamers are attached to the haraigushi, which is waved to the left, right, and left. Other implements used in harae include the *ônusa*, a branch of the sacred sakaki tree or other evergreen to which linen or paper streamers are attached, and the *konusa*, a smaller version used for self-purification by the individual.

Presentation of the sacred sakaki branch to the kami, called tamagushi, is one of the most common acts of formal worship at a shrine. The worshiper receives the offering from the priest. The worshiper proceeds to the offering table in a reverent attitude and begins the proper actions that bless the kami. The worshiper steps forward and places the tamagushi on the offering table, steps back, and bows twice, claps twice, and then makes a final bow. Tamagushi can be performed any time the shrine is open and the priest is present.

Shinto Purification Ceremonies

Prayers are offered for the removal of all sin, pollution, and misfortune. The body and mind are purified and restored to a condition worthy of approaching the gods. The traditional spelling is harae, but today the word is usually spelled harai. Harae is performed at the beginning of all religious ceremonies and whenever a specific need arises. In ancient times, two types of harae, called *yoshi-harae* and *ashi-harae* (literally, purification of good and purification of evil), appear to have been performed, but the meaning of the two terms is not clear.

Harae is one of the most important ceremonies in Shinto, and various forms of it have developed. For example, *Nagoshi-no-Oharai* is a purification performed on the last day of the sixth month of the lunar calendar; it marks the middle of the year. *Minohi no harae* is a type of purification performed on days of the snake in the third month of the lunar calendar. *Shubatsu* is a harae ceremony performed by priests before a ceremony or religious rite. Priests also perform a special purification rite called *kessai* before officiating at major religious ceremonies.

The origin of harae is described in the *Kojiki* story of the god Izanagi no mikoto, who is said to have washed in order to remove the pollution of death after visiting his wife in the land of the dead (yomi). Izanagi went to visit her there but broke a taboo and was forced to part with her. Having come in contact with pollution, he feared that misfortune would result, and so went to the sea and purified himself. One term for pollution was *kagare*, which could be translated "inauspicious." This pollution was seen as the reason for unhappiness or evil, and was considered an impediment to religious ceremonies. Pollution could disqualify a person from participating in religious rites and social life for a certain period of time. It could be removed by performing ceremonies of exorcism or purification. Pollution was of sufficient importance to merit a number of different terms to refer to it (*tsumi, imi, kibuku*). Until the middle ages, all of the following were regarded as sources of pollution: the death of humans and domestic animals, childbirth, menstruation, eating meat, and illness. In modern times the emphasis falls on mental or spiritual pollution.

Ôharae

The *Ôharae* ("The Great Purification") is a very important ceremony. It is performed twice a year nationwide, on the last days of June and of December, and also on other occasions when deemed necessary. Shinto not only provides a means for the sins, pollutions, and misfortunes of an individual to be removed, but also provides a way for evil and misfortune to be removed from an entire nation. These rituals also renew life and bring down the blessings of the gods. The norito used at the Ôharae is called *Ôbarae no kotoba.* (There is also a common practice of reciting the Obarae no kotoba, either alone or in unison, with slight changes.) The Obarae no kotoba is regarded as a sacred liturgy. It was the duty of the Nakatomi clan to recite it, and so it is also called by the name *Nakatomi no harae.*

Misogi-harae

Misogi-harae is linked to the same *Kojiki* myth as was described above, namely, the story of Izanagi's purification in the river after becoming polluted in the land of death. Misogi is a Shrine Shinto ritual that involves both priests and shrine members in a very rigorous form of purification. As performed at Tsubaki Grand Shrine, Misogi-harae seems to combine Shinto's earliest water purification ritual with esoteric practices from mountain asceticism (hand *mudras*, signs, and word-symbols). The following inclusion of Chief Priest (*Guji*) Yamamoto's description will give the reader some impression of the many complicated elements found in this ritual. Nothing, however, can quite prepare one for the actual experience of stepping under an icy waterfall in the context of *kami-ki* (the potential experience of divine power).

MISOGI AND SPIRITUAL EXERCISES [83]
Before Misogi

The mind and body should be conditioned before misogi. On the night before, it is recommended that participants abstain from eating meat or drinking alcohol. The senses should be freed by avoiding any physical substances that might cloud or distort them; they should be prepared to be receptive.

Preparation

Those taking part assemble in front of the Shrine office at the agreed time, and from there they proceed into the hall beside the *haiden* to receive a simplified form of oharae called shubatsu. Since the waterfall, which is called *Konryu Myôjin* (*Myôjin* means "gracious kami") is a kami, there is need for purification before entering. Thereafter, we move to the dressing rooms where men don white loincloths and *hachimakis* (headbands) and women don long white kimono-like robes and hachimakis. After coming out of the dressing areas, we move down to an open area above the entrance to the waterfall and face the honden, or inner sanctuary. We bow twice, clap twice, and bow once. We are now ready to commence the warm-up exercises.

Exercise I: *Furitama* (Soul Shaking)

(1) Stand with your legs about shoulder width apart. (2) Place your hands together with the right hand over the left. Leave space between them big enough for an imaginary ping-pong ball. (3) Place your hands in that position in front of your stomach and shake them vigorously up and down. (4) While shaking them concentrate and repeat the words: *Harae-do-no-Okami*—an invocation to the kami of the place of harae.

The Object of Exercise I

The purpose of shaking the soul is to generate awareness of it within yourself. In Shinto, *kon* (the soul) is one of the four important elements along with mei (life), rei (spirit), and ki (energy). Kon is the most important of the four since human beings can also be described as *waketama* (separated individual souls), which is another way of saying "children of the kami."

Exercise II *Torifune* (Bird Rowing)

(1) Stand up straight and put your left leg forward. (2) Clench both fists with your thumbs inside. (3) Lean forward and move your arms as though rowing a boat; starting from your left knee and ending near your armpits. As you "row," shout "*Yie.*" (4) Perform this twenty times and then repeat Furitama. (5) Changing to a right leg stance, repeat the Torifune shouting "*Ei*" and "*Ho*" alternately. Do this twenty times and then repeat Furitama. (6) Return to the left foot forward stance and remake the clenched fists as before and bring the hands up to the chest to a shout of "Yie" and thrust them down and forward with hands opened and fingers extended to a shout of "*Se.*" After this, once again repeat the Furitama.

The Object of Exercise II

The purpose of Exercise II is to introduce a dimension of

physical calisthenics along with the spiritual. Since misogi is a psycho-physical experience, both types of warm-up exercises are necessary.

Exercise III *Otakebi* (Shouting)
(1) Stand up straight leaving a space between your feet. (2) Place your hands on your hips. (3) Follow the *michihiko*, leader, as he shouts the following three invocations: *Iku-tama! Taru-tama! Tama-tamaru-tama!* (4) Follow him in repeating three times the long invocation: *Okami! Okami! Kunitsu-Okami! Sarutahiko Okami To-toshi-ya.*

The Object of Exercise III
Shouting *Iku-tama* activates the soul that is just coming to awareness. *Taru-tama* affirms that one can realize the infinite in one's own soul. *Tama-tamaru-tama* confirms both of the preceding invocations and keeps the soul activated at an elevated level. The closing invocation addresses *Sarutahiko Okami*, head of the earthly kami and acknowledges him to be of great power.

Exercise IV *Okorobi* (Yielding)
(1) Stand as in Exercise III. (2) Place the left hand on your hip and your hand with two fingers extended in a gesture that resembles the "Boy Scout Salute." (3) Three kami are invoked here and with each invocation, you cut the air in a sweeping gesture with the right hand as follows: *Kunitoko-tachi-no-Mikoto! Yie! Sarutahiko-no-Okami! Yie! Kokuryu-no-Okami! Yie!* At each time of cutting the air, you should take a step forward with your left foot and then back again.

The Object of Exercise IV
By specifying these three important kami, *Kunitokotachi-no-Mikoto* (the earthly kami), *Sarutahiko Okami* (kami of guidance and head of the earthly kami), and *Kokuryuon-no-Okami* (kami of water, life, and ki), you can be united with them, remove your impurities, and receive their power as your own.

Exercise V *Ibuki* (Breathing)

(1) Stand with your feet apart. (2) Lower your hands and arms toward your knees. (3) Lift your arms above your head by extending them fully outwards. (4) Inhale while raising them. (5) Exhale slowly and deliberately while lowering your hands again. (6) Place hands and arms down by knees and exhale completely. (7) Repeat five times. (8) Turn to face the waterfall, bow twice, clap twice, and open your palms upwards towards the fall. (9) You are now ready to go down the steps toward the waterfall.

The Object of Exercise V

The purpose is to conclude the preparation by taking deep breaths, which have the effect of raising the metabolism of the ki to its highest level of sensitivity and receptivity by absorbing the ki of the universe.

Exercise VI *Nyusui* (Getting into the Water)

(1) Just prior to entering the water, you will receive *Sakashio*, or purifying salt, from the michihiko (leader). It will be sprinkled on you. (2) Receive a ladle with Japanese sake and salt. Spray it from your mouth in three mouthfuls into the stream. (3) The michihiko will recite the nine-letter prayer as follows: *Rin-Pyo-To-Sha-Kai-Zin-Retsu-Zai-Zen* (1 2 3 4 5 6 7 8 9). (4) The michihiko then cuts the air symbolically nine times, and shouts "Yei!" (In Shinto, the numbers from one to nine symbolize the secular world and its impurities. The cutting of the air symbolizes removing the impurities of existence from its nine areas.) (5) Enter the water and spray water on your face, chest, and loins. (6) Clap your hands twice, and bow once. (7) Cut the air from right to left with your right hand as in Exercise IV. (8) Approach the waterfall and enter, right shoulder first. Turn round and face the michihiko holding your hands in front with middle fingers together pointing away from you. (9) Shout the following: *Harae-tamae-Kiyome-tamae-ro-kon-sho-jo*!

The Meaning of the Final Prayer: The expressions harae and *kiyome* ask for the purifying of the individual by the washing away of all tsumi from the *ro-kon-sho-jo*, that is, from the six elements of human beings that Shinto identified (the five senses and the mind).

After misogi, participants go back to the haiden and dry off. They then participate in a period of *chinkon-sai*, spiritual practice, to pacify the soul. This in turn is followed by a *naorai*, a ceremonial drinking with the kami, which has the effect of strengthening the vertical *musubi* (creativity). The connections between kami and human being, as well as between one human being and another, intensify. Persons in relation to both kami and other persons can begin to understand and become what destiny decreed they should be at birth. This is the goal and ideal of misogi, and ultimately of Shinto itself.

SUMMARY ABOUT RITUALS AND SACRED ACTION

Most persons in the twentieth century want "instant spirituality." They do not look with favor on hours and hours of dancing, drumming, chanting, or waterfall purification (misogi). But objections to the time requirements of action-centered religion are of the same order as objections to its lack of intellectual sophistication; both are irrelevant. Because this type of religious experience works in the here-and-now—in the present time of doing and acting—the longer the activity lasts, the better. Furthermore, acting and doing are a way around *the thinking, doubting mind*— so the experience is to be judged on its own merits. We know that members of a group bond more easily by doing something together than they would by studying a doctrine. Group activity leads to group solidarity. This is not to say that there are not other, more appropriate, ways to judge ritual. One can say that the experience was weak or ugly, without psychological and spiritual power, and so on—such judgments are appropriate for action-centered religion. If a ritual lacks beauty and power, it may be judged worthless.

Action-Centered Religion and Ethics

There are a number of ethical principles encoded in Shinto's rituals. Through the invocation to kami, one learns that spiritual entities can be experienced anywhere. Shinto ritual also demonstrates that pleasure is good, community is primary, and life is interconnected. Shinto ritual teaches community members how to act. Shinto ethics teaches the ancient and sacred words (*kotodama*): *Sei, Mei, Shô, Jiki*: Be purified . . . practice cleanliness . . . don't tell a lie . . . be cheerful . . .

These may seem to be very simple ethical notions. Nevertheless, they are very powerful. They suggest a collective ethic that is world- and life-affirming, and optimistic. Individuals find their place in the community by trying their hardest without complaining. Cleanliness and orderliness are next to godliness. Any transgressions are viewed as impurities that create disharmony in the community. These must be removed by communal action—the rituals that dissolve the pollution and restore pure living.

5

Sacred Space

Protect me in the night.
Protect me and shelter me in the day.
Grant me happiness.
With awe and reverence, I humbly speak these words.

—Prayer of Inari

SHINTO SHRINES

P art of being modern and secular is to have no holy places, no sacred spaces where one is overcome with awe, fear, dread, fascination, and excitement. Even a growing number of Japanese no longer experience "kami-ness" in time or space. Yet there is no way to understand Shinto shrines except as sacred spaces.

We will begin with a look at the land as sacred, then shrines, and finally home shrines. This is not a guided tour but an imagined pilgrimage to places in Japan where a heightened sense of "kami-ness" is present. Anything less would be a fraud, for the spirituality of Shinto depends on a sensate experience of the divine in the world. (I am not naively forgetting that "religion" is also about business, social functioning, identity formation, and politics. But to avoid looking at Shinto's claim to experience kami in specific locations would be to arrogantly ignore Shinto's unique claims.)

MARKING OFF SACRED SPACE

Sacred space is marked off in a variety of ways in Shinto. The most obvious ways to mark a place as sacred are with a *torii* (an entryway) and a *shimenawa* (a sacred rope).

Torii (literally "a bird perch")

Torii is a distinctive arch or gateway erected at the entrance to the sacred precincts of a shrine that separates the inner area from the profane world surrounding it. Torii may also be erected along the avenue of approach to a shrine.

Shimenawa

This rope separates sacred from profane and hearkens back to Amaterasu's being prevented from returning to the rock cave and plunging the world back into darkness.

These mark the sacred space of a shrine in established or organized forms of Shinto (in Shrine, Sectarian, Imperial Household, and State forms of Shinto). Sacred space within a home, and sometimes in a business as well, is demarcated by a

Built at the approach to a Shinto shrine, a torii separates the sacred world from the profane world.

Shimenawa are sacred ropes that are hung in front of worship halls, altars, and across the entrance to Shinto shrines.

high shelf called a kamidana. We will explore three locations of sacred space: Japan, the shrine, and the family altar.

JAPAN AS SACRED SPACE

There are many places in Japan that might be considered awe-inspiring—the sacred waterfalls, the holy forest, and the many divine mountain peaks—but the most awesome is Mount Fuji. But how can a mere mountain be thought to represent the divine, or the divine indwelling in nature, or even the perception that nature itself is divine? In response to that question, allow me to tell you a story.

A number of years ago I was en route to Japan to make a film about Buddhism. A beautiful young Japanese woman was seated beside me during the long flight to Tokyo. But the introduction went poorly. She had just graduated from Mills College in Oakland, California, and had no interest in talking with a religious studies professor. She said she was an atheist, and she particularly despised Japanese religion. Not another word was said until we saw Mt. Fuji. Usually surrounded in clouds, Mt. Fuji was adorned that day in the glow of the setting sun. It was resplendent. There was an audible gasp at its beauty from my seatmate. I remarked: "Ah, that old mountain. There are so many more beautiful in the world that I don't understand what people see in it." I enjoyed the horror in her shocked expression. I could hardly hold back my laughter. Then I confessed: "See. You are religious after all! You reverence nature." She instantly understood a different meaning for the word "religion." She had rejected much about religion, especially its business aspects. But she certainly experienced the awe of this place, the in-break of the sacred into time and space. Nature itself seemed to her as divine. In the next twenty minutes, before the plane touched down, she talked about her Shinto father and her Buddhist mother. She spoke directly about my favorite shrines and places, the very ones that I had experienced as sacred while visiting Japan. Her father had wanted to take her to each of these, confirming my choices. I was barely able to say goodbye and focus on finding my luggage.

Many Japanese believe their land to be the "land of the gods, the land of the kami." They hike to the top of mountains not so much for exercise or recreation, but as a pilgrimage to sacred spots. There are many routes that have attracted pilgrims. Many have their own names.

Japanese adorn their homes with art about, and objects from, these sacred places. Fuji-san or Fujiyama may be the most popular subject of this artwork.

There are sacred localities such as Ise, Isumo, Miyajima, and hundreds more. Even the village is sacred as the home of the *ujikami* (clan kami) or the founding ancestor of the locality.

THE SHRINE AS SACRED SPACE
Visiting a Shrine

There are two contrasting attitudes about the fundamental nature of a Shinto shrine. The first is reflected in the basic call to worship[84] that is performed every morning in shrines across Japan. The kami are called "down" to be present at the celebration or recitation of the prayers (norito), where they will receive praise and offerings. Then their "return" is acknowledged (or directed). In other words, the kami are not present on a permanent basis—they come and go.

The second attitude is reflected in the notion of enshrined kami. Except during the height of the Buddhist-Shinto synthesis, Shinto has resisted the use of images to represent the kami. However, Shinto does make use of sacred objects called goshintai (or shintai).[85] They are symbols or signs of the kami, and the spirit (tama) of the kami is said to reside in them. Examples of goshintai include mirrors, jewels, even swords. These are housed in a hidden area of the shrine and almost never seen.[86]

VISITING TSUBAKI GRAND SHRINE

The map on page 79 is of the Tsubaki Grand Shrine, which is located on the Ise Peninsula, near Osaka, Japan. The numbers in the following text correspond to the numbers on the map and will indicate the route one might take when visiting this shrine. In addition, objects on the map are italicized in the text.

The approaches to a Shinto shrine (jinja) are marked by *torii* (1), "bird perches," which separate the sacred from the profane. There may be only one or two torii or many, as at Tsubaki Dai

SACRED SPACE

Ancient Shinto had no permanent shrine buildings at all. The experience of the kami as divine or sacred could be anywhere—anywhere in Japan, that is! The myths made that very clear. Japan was the "Land of the Kami" and was referred to as such in the earliest Chinese documents describing Chinese contact with these mysterious islands. Only after contact with the mainland cultures of Korea and China did Shinto begin to build shrines for the kami.

The Japanese did not seem to reflect on their divinization of the land—their islands—until there had been contact with the West; first Portugal and then Holland. Shinto myths were subjected to national needs. There emerged the idea of the sacred nation personified by the emperor; and it was for that sacred nation that Japanese subjects were to be ready to sacrifice even their lives in times of military conflict. Thus, a latent warrior religion evolved out of the earlier, less rationalized, but more complex experience of sacred space.

The more ancient manner of experiencing special places (such as majestic mountains or tiny islands) as homes of the kami has never been lost. Gradually these places were set aside and made into permanent shrines with buildings and consecrated space. The sacred compound, the shrine, would become the principal means of experiencing sacred space. At first, there was no compound at all—just a natural object like a waterfall or a mountain formation that elicited the emotions of holiness and awe. Gradually, however, shrine complexes, with buildings, entranceways, and special man-made objects or images, came to seem necessary as homes, temporary or permanent, for the kami.

The most personal sacred space would be the kamidana, the so-called "god-shelf" found in most homes in Japan. Homes, too, needed their own sacred area. These home shrines invited the experience of kami-ness into family life and daily activity.

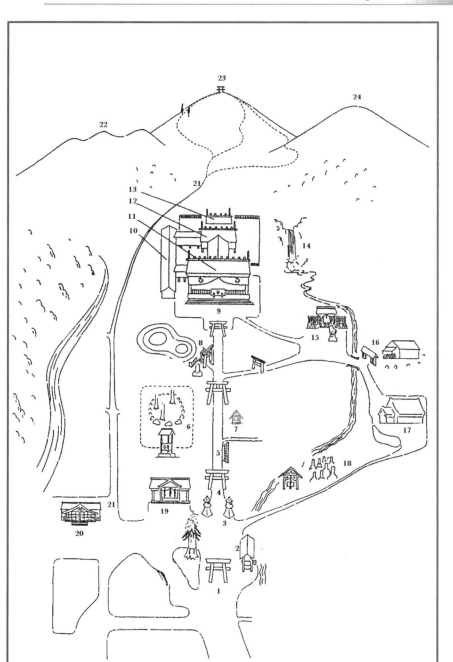

Map of Tsubaki Grand Shrine, Ise Peninsula, Japan.

Jinja. Before passing through the torii, the first stop is the *temizu-ya* (2), the purification pavilion, where the visitor washes his or her hands and mouth, ladling water first on the left hand, then on the right. A final scoop pours water in the left hand from which to rinse the mouth. Waste water is poured in front of the fresh water trough (never back into it) and the visitor proceeds through the great gate, or torii, up the pathway to the main complex. With this ritual cleansing of hands and mouth (temizu), one is ready to enter sacred space.

Along the way are *toro* or stone lanterns (3), a Chinese influence, to light the way at night. There will surely be Korean lion-dogs, *Koma-inu* or *Shishi-koma-inu*—they act as protectors and keep away evil and misfortune. By the time we notice the lanterns and lion-dog guardians we are on the *Omote Sandô* (4), the main approach to the Shrine. There will be more torii and enormous trees lining the path. A little farther there is a *Donor's List* (5). Good works do not go unnoticed and having one's name in a sacred place seems to be a multicultural desire. Almost unnoticed on the left is one of the most important sites in Japan. It is *Iwakura no Mifune* (6), the landing site of Ninigi no Mikoto, the grandson of the Sun Goddess, Amaterasu Ômikami. This connects the sacred stories found in the *Kojiki* and the *Nihonshoki* with an actual place in Japan, making this spot one of the most sacred in Japan. [My own research leads me to think that imperial mythology has been superimposed on Tsubaki's unique local stories. This landing place was once seacoast and possibly the landing site of the pioneer explorer god, Sarutahiko, a giant with a huge nose (compared to the indigenous people, perhaps). But in the imperial mythology, Sarutahiko is the earth ruler whose claim has to be nullified so that Ninigi, grandson of Amaterasu Ômikami, can begin the imperial line with the Yamato clan.]

A few yards farther on the right are statues of *Ebisu* and *Daikoku* (7). Suddenly we have shifted from the worlds of imperial history and mythology to Folk Shinto. Ebisu (also known as Kotoshironushi no kami) is a kami. He is protector

Iwakura no Mifune—Landing Site of Ninigi no Mikoto
(stop #6 on map).

of the rice fields and also of fishing. He was believed to have
come from the sea—from a faraway country. Now he joins with
Daikoku as a protector of prosperity and happiness. Daikoku
(also known as Ôkuninushi no kami) evolved from Mahâkâla
(Indian deity of Great Time); transported to Japan during the
middle ages by Esoteric Buddhism. Daikoku became known
as the god of agriculture. Folk Shinto merged elements from
Japan's agricultural past with more developed notions borrowed
from the mainland: China and Korea, but also India.

About halfway up the *Omote Sandô* (4), the main approach
to the Shrine, is the burial mound of *Sarutahiko Okami* (8).
Even guided tours by the shrine priests may leave this site
unnoticed, not because it is unimportant, but because it will

Statues of *Ebisu and Daikoku* (stop #7 on map).

require too much explanation. Two things stand out. First, as a general rule there are no burial sites within the sacred space of a Shinto shrine. Second, this is a burial mound, linking it to practices that are nearly two millennia old. (I have discussed this site at length with Tsubaki Grand Shrine's chief priest, Guji Yukitaka Yamamoto. I have asked him the unthinkable: Would it be possible to excavate the burial mound? It is so sacred that this was quickly pronounced impossible and one of the most barbarian things that he had ever heard. Yet this mound is a bridge between history and mythology. Was Sarutahiko a real

Jinja Shaden, or shrine buildings (stop #9 on the map).

explorer who immigrated to Japan—the pioneer navigator who landed at this site and was buried here? Would this mound provide links to Southeast Asia or to a northern point of origin? Would there be DNA that would also help to locate Japan's ancestry? Of course these are historical questions that might even threaten the sacred stories as told in the *Kojiki* and the *Nihonshoki.*)

We now arrive at the front of the *Jinja Shaden,* the shrine buildings (9). The walk up the *Omote Sandô* (4) was nearly a half mile beneath towering trees and through numerous torii before reaching the main shrine buildings. There is a place for an offering, with a rope to ring a bell to announce a gift, but this is only for those who are in a hurry. There is a subtle barrier that points out that the entrance into the shrine complex is at the left. Along the way into the shrine are stalls with miko (temple maidens) selling talismans and mementos. The *Shamushô* (10) or shrine offices allow the visitor to register and obtain the services of a shrine priest. Many come for a specific ritual such as the announcement of the birth of a child or its presentation to the kami on a special occasion. These rituals are done in the main three buildings in the shrine. The first is the *heiden* (11), the Outer Sanctuary or hall of offerings. The heiden is also called Kagura-den (kagura, a performance of classical dance and music) because it is there that one can have these ceremonies performed, celebrating some of life's most important events and doing something that is especially pleasing to the kami. The miko dance is a symbolic reminder of the time that Uzume, kami of entertainment and literature, danced in such a hilarious way that Amaterasu was drawn out from the cave and light was restored to the universe.

More formal rituals and ceremonies are held in the *haiden* or Worship Hall (12). This hall like the others in a shrine complex is made of the most beautiful wood in an ancient architecture that is as simple as it is beautiful. Unusual beauty is a primary characteristic of the sacred, of kami. Implements of worship found in the haiden include the haraigushi, or purification wand, various drums, altars, and offerings of sake and large sacks of rice—but not so many items that the overall effect of simplicity, order, and beauty is lost.

Only after a ceremony in the haiden is one purified enough to be invited to a special celebration that approaches the holiest place in the shrine, the *honden* or Inner Sanctuary (13). The honden is also called the Shinden or hall of the kami because the goshintai, the object in which the spirit of the kami is believed to reside, is kept here. The honden is relatively small and houses the enshrined spirit (*mitama* or tama) of the kami. This cannot be viewed except by the most senior priest of the shrine during special private rituals.

While the *gohei* represents the presence of the kami during worship, shintai or goshintai are objects within the honden in which the Kami are said to reside. The object may be a mirror, or sword, or a treasure of great beauty. This is the most holy area of the shrine and should remain hidden from view.

However, the worshiper does come quite close to the honden to accept consecrated sake and a sweet, a communion with the kami. This usually completes a formal visit to the shrine, unless there is a special need such as a consultation about business or family matters. These are done in private rooms for counseling. One is then free to walk around the grounds, dine or picnic, take pictures, and buy religious materials or talismans (*omimori*).

There are two waterfalls within the shrine precinct. The *Konryu Myôjin* waterfall (14) is the one currently used for an ancient practice called *misogi shuhô*. Since it is mentioned in the Shinto Classics, misogi must be at least thirteen hundred years old. In the *Kojiki* and *Nihonshoki*, the divine parent-kami, Izanagi, washed away the pollution from the land of the dead, Yomi, by doing misogi. There are associations (*kô*) of shrine members who gather monthly (these are local members) or on special occasions to do misogi. This is a practice that seems to have been done much more in the past than in modern times, but Tsubaki Shinto promotes this practice both to please the kami and for benefits of health and prosperity. It is a major purification practice that uses the symbolism of cold water cleansing to suggest a purification of mind and life that more closely follows the kami way.

As one leaves the main shrine to Sarutahiko Okami, one finds a secondary shrine to *Ame-uzume-no-mikoto* (15). Technically, this shrine only holds the divided spirit (mitama) of Uzume, goddess or kami of entertainment and literature. Whatever the technicality, this is one of the more important places for her reverence in all of Japan. Entertainers of all professions, some so famous that their pictures grace the business office after their visit, come to ensure success and

Konryu Myôjin waterfall (stop #14 on the map).

prosperity. Of course, rituals are available from priests and miko who serve this shrine.

At the end of this side path is the *Reisho-an*, a traditional tea house (16). It is dedicated to one of Tsubaki's past supporters, Konosuke Matsushita, founder of the Matsushita Corporation.

Turning right along that path one comes to the *Gyômandô* (17). This is a reminder of Tsubaki's adaptation during the

***Reisho-an,* a traditional tea house (stop #16 on the map).**

centuries that Buddhism dominated religious affairs. The Gyômandô is a Dual Shinto-Buddhist temple where Shinto and Buddhism are combined, kami and Buddhas or boddhisattvas are equated, and ancient esoteric Buddhist rituals are performed. The sacred space of the Gyômandô is qualitatively different from the rest of the shrine, which demonstrates how Shrine Shinto and Dual Shinto are simultaneously separate and overlapping. In addition to esoteric fire ceremonies, one can find here an enshrinement of the soul or spirit (tama) of important shrine supporters, possibly a mixture of the practice of enshrining the spirit of the clan kami (ujigami) with ancestor worship.

Turning back toward the main pathway, one sees the *Enmei Jizo-do* (18). Again the stereotypes about Shinto must be sacrificed in order to understand its reality. Jizo are Buddhist statues to a boddhisattva of mercy, the protector of children who died at birth or in infancy. But there is even more here.

There is pure history here as well. There are memorial towers and markers of a battleground commemorating more than

Enmei Jizo-do (stop #18 on the map).

four hundred fallen warrior-priests, both Buddhist and Shinto, who fought a shogun during the Oda wars of the sixteenth century. At that time, Tsubaki Grand Shrine was the defending shrine on the imperial road down the peninsula to Ise Grand Shrine. It included six Buddhist temples and one of Japan's most important Dual Shinto complexes. The Shogun Oda Nobunaga could not tolerate its independent power so his army attacked, destroyed Tsubaki, and killed all of its priest-defenders. A later shogun helped rebuild a much smaller shrine.

When one returns to the main entrance (1), one notices the *Shishi-do* or *Lion Hall* (19) to the left. Most visitors will proceed along the *Omote Sandô* (4), as we did, ignoring the Shishi-do. It is interesting to note that the Shishi-do is dedicated to practices that are associated with Folk Shinto, such as the blessing of new objects. In the past, the objects blessed might have been livestock, but in modern Japan people come to the Shishi-do to have their cars blessed and to receive a talisman to hang from the rearview mirror or put on the dash to protect against accidents. (At one time the young priests of the shrine were having so many traffic accidents that the chief priest admonished them; he asked how they could drive so poorly if they had the blessings of the Shishi-do.)

One of many shrines along the trail (stop #21 on the map).

Leaving the enclosed and sacred grounds of the shrine proper we come to the *Sanshuden* or Guest House (20). In addition to being a full-service hotel, the Sanshuden is used as a hotel and reception center for the many Shinto weddings at the shrine. One of its many features is the Japanese bath or *ofuro*.

Originating beside the Sanshuden are trails that lead up the mountain to shrines (21) at the peaks *Kunimi* (22), *Nyuodogatake* (23), and *Tsubaki* (24). One of the most fascinating events in the shrine's calendar is the hike to the summit of Mount

Nyuodogatake. What is amazing is to see sixty-year-old shrine members or ko pilgrims making the arduous trek up this steep mountain. At the top, there is a ritual to the kami and a celebration with feasting and sharing in sacred sake.

Our tour of the sacred space of one shrine cannot adequately convey the beauty and power of Shinto shrines. But it does make us at least a little more familiar with them. It also illustrates that visiting a shrine is second only to participating in the rituals in having some sense of the diversity of Shrine Shinto and of its overlap with other types of Shinto. [87]

THE HOME ALTAR AS SACRED SPACE

The family shrine often contains sacred objects consecrated by a priest and housed within a miniature honden. As a result of the consecration, the family shrine has technically received the divided soul (tama) of the enshrined kami. It will require daily worship. The family will need someone to do this regularly and properly.

Perhaps of even greater importance, the family shrine houses the spirits of the deceased relatives. They too are reverenced with prayers and offerings of water and sake and tiny amounts of salt, rice, raw fruit or vegetables, and cooked foods. Fresh flowers are also placed on the altar when available.

Ancestor reverence at the kamidana is done daily, on special anniversaries of the individual deceased, and at special times of family struggle or celebration.

A shimenawa or sacred rope reminds the worshiper that this is sacred space. One may be reminded of the sacred story of Amaterasu being enticed from the rock cave by Uzume's dance and being prevented from going back in by the shimenawa.

A miniature shrine houses the enshrined divided kami spirit (tama) and its goshintai, or sacred object that symbolizes the presence of the kami in this home. The vases hold sakaki branches, holy to the kami. Beautiful cut or potted flowers can be substituted. Food offerings of fresh fruit and vegetables as well as salt and sake are a daily necessity. There may be

A kamidana (home altar).

amulets (omimori) from visits to shrines like Ise Grand Shrine that connect this sacred space to pilgrimage spots around Japan.

Ancestor tablets, usually placed in a lower position, are also reverenced. Like all sacred spaces, this one must be cared for, be orderly and clean, and be beautiful.

6

Sacred Time

Longing as I do
For a sight of thee,
Now that I have arrived here,
Even thus do I long
Desirous of a sight of thee!

— Saimei Tenno, *Nihonshoki*, Book XXVI

S acred time is most difficult to study because our modern experience has demythologized time and made it fully secular. This is happening so rapidly in Japan that much of this chapter will be a museum piece, although Japan is still rich with artifacts about sacred time saved in its calendar, its public festivals, and even in the life-cycle events already seen by most as secular (as having nothing to do with religion).

Sacred time involves a time out of ordinary time. Sacred time will be defined as mythic time—a symbolic time when actions, words, and presence might be experienced as sacred or not ordinary. One may induce this "time out" with sacred action, sacred words, sacred presence, or any combination of these. Or there may be an in-break of sacred time much as a gift. In Shinto, it is most likely that the experience of sacred time will come at a festival (matsuri), when the solemn and chaotic powers of participation in community seem most likely to alter ordinary time. Sacred time seems less likely to be experienced in casual visits to shrines, in shrine entertainments such as dance (kagura) or drama (*nô*), or even during visits to be in the shrine's natural setting—simply because modern life has so many activities that compete and make Shinto's religious experiences seem ordinary.

Mythological time is closely related to mythic time. It is time as portrayed in the mythology of a people, and mythologies generally narrate events that happened in mythic time. Mythological time is an aspect of mythic time—since mythology recounts stories in which and through which sacred time may be experienced.

The second part of the chapter will be about historical time (one aspect of ordinary time). At least in theory, there should be no tension between sacred and historic time in Shinto. In the Japanese Classics, the *Kojiki* and the *Nihonshoki*, mythological time runs into historical time seamlessly—if one allows the imperial spin on history to stand.[88]

MYTHOLOGICAL TIME

Before looking at sacred time as patterned by the calendar year, let's take a detour into mythological time. Mythological time is a time out of the ordinary, or "a time out of (ordinary) time." Shinto's mythological time is the age of the gods (Kami-yo). Is the age of the gods to be understood literally or metaphorically? Mythology taken literally contradicts the very nature of mythic time as a "time out of time," so it is important to recognize that myths use language in a non-ordinary fashion—symbolically. A symbolic description of something points not to its empirical qualities alone, but to its entire spiritual nature. Sacred things can only be spoken about by using language symbolically.

The Japanese Classics and the entire oral tradition of Shinto look to a time of beginnings, the age of the gods (Kami-yo). It

SACRED TIME, LIFE-CYCLE EVENTS, AND CRISIS MINISTRY

The life-cycle events performed by Shinto priests are generally celebrations. These happy events range from births, presentations of newborns to kami and the shrine community, coming-of-age rituals, weddings (this is Shinto's ultimate ministry), and many lesser life-cycle events. What is paradoxical is how poorly Shrine Shinto ministers to failures, suffering, and death. Those who experience such life traumas often turn to Sectarian Shinto groups or Buddhist or Christian alternatives.

Shinto's cosmology includes the idea of the harmony of order and chaos, of good and evil. Such a cosmology should have led to rituals for the restoration of harmony, and to bring comfort to those distressed by life's events. But government interference during the Tokugawa era as well as during the Restoration resulted in ministry and rituals for life's suffering being assigned to Buddhism. Consequently, when its members experience life's crises, Shinto appears only half a religion. One test of how well Shinto is able to make use of its new freedom from government restraint will be whether it develops rituals of compassion for use at times of suffering and death.

Recently a new generation of Shinto priests has begun practicing pastoral counseling. They even perform rituals for funerals, ones that go beyond the tradition of enshrining the tama or soul of the deceased ancestor. If this trend continues, Shrine Shinto will be well on its way to ministering to the fullness of human life, with rituals for life's traumas and pain as well as rituals of celebration.

was a time of generation and creativity (musubi). Creation unfolds in sacred time in a highly symbolic way, quite unnatural from the viewpoint of ordinary time. Yet it is a time when order, harmony, purity, power, courage, loyalty, and other virtues are unfolding. But that is only one dimension. There is also chaos, conflict, pollution, fear, deceit, and similar flaws. In Shinto mythology, this creative process is illustrated by both positive and negative examples among the kami. Whereas other mythologies locate the primeval struggle in a battle between gods and demons, Shinto places that struggle at the very heart of creation—in kami-ness.

What is missing (by comparison with other mythologies) is a dichotomy between good and evil. The creative process in the Kami-yo—in sacred time—encompasses the dynamics of order and chaos, harmony and strife, purity and impurity. They seem to unfold much like the agricultural year—according to seasons of new life, growth, harvest, and death. The cycles return year after year (cyclical time)[89]—but only when care is exercised to do things at their proper time (sacred time) and in their proper way (sacred action).

As an action-centered religion, Shinto focuses on the "here and now," the present moment. It does look back to a "past" that remembers what the "gods" (kami) did "in the beginning," but it brings that past into the present moment of ritual. This is a past that is, paradoxically, present. It is present because it is reenacted in ritual, festival, and dance. Shinto has only a vague concern with the future. Its sacred time is centered in what may be described as either the eternal "now" (because the sacred time of the beginning is always brought forward into the present moment, and the present moment is always reconnected to the sacred time of the beginning), or as the cyclically returning "now" (because the sacred time of the beginning and the present moment are merged through cyclically recurring rituals and festivals).

Mythic memory is not the same as historical memory. There may be some history embedded in Shinto myths (as in the account of Sarutahiko Okami landing at the head of the Ise Peninsula by boat and later dying there and being buried in a mound—kami are not supposed to die on earth). However, recounting history is only one small part of what myths do; it is not a very significant aspect of their purpose. The primary purpose of a myth is to depict mythic time. Mythic time is cyclic and symbolic. It is the symbol that reveals the meaning, purpose, and mystery of the myth, and therefore it is the symbol that allows the myth to function as a model for human behavior. When mythic time is literalized, and read as historical time, its symbolic dimension is lost. When myth is read literally, it collapses into the unreal, the implausible, and the nonsensical. Unless myths are interpreted through the living symbols and metaphors that bring the reader or hearer into sacred time, they risk being turned into silly, childish tales—not worth the time and effort it takes to get through them.

Yet, paradoxically, there are times when literalism is an avenue to mythic time. The Shinto child will experience the sacred stories literally, and yet he or she will gain entry into sacred time. Because the barrier between the sacred and the ordinary is more porous for a child, children can more easily make the journey from the literal statement to its mythic destination. Indeed, in terms of cognitive development that is the child's only possibility. An adult, however, has additional capabilities of reasoning and reflective thinking. At the adult level of cognition, limiting the experience of mythic time to its literal dimensions subtracts rather than adds to its meaning and wonder. Just as the kami are both good and bad at times, so Shinto combines and harmonizes mythology's literal appearance with its symbolic meaning to open up the possibility of finding awe, wonder, and ecstasy (ecstasy literally means "standing outside of ordinary time").

It is in the crossroads of ritual and story and sacred time that Shinto springs to life and attains its full power to transform lives. The awesome convergence of sacred story (myth), sacred action (ritual), and sacred time (festivals) enables those who are receptive to enter the sacred time "in the beginning," to stand before the powers that created heaven and earth, and to experience a new birth.

SHINTO MYTH, RITUAL, AND FESTIVAL

Professor Keiichi Yanagawa, an old friend, began his essay on "The Sensation of Matsuri"[90] by comparing a Shinto festival (matsuri) with his Japanese university's demonstrations and riots in 1968—both were a kind of "time out of time," when one could not do the things that one did in ordinary time. Only when it was all over could one return to ordinary time and mundane reality. Yanagawa reviewed some of the studies of matsuri and concluded that each of them missed whatever it was that made a festival a festival. Some of the studies reduced matsuri to its history, others to its social and psychological functions, and still others (those who were structuralists) reduced matsuri to a set of dualism or opposing terms. In analyzing myths and texts, structuralists look for opposing terms that follow their own trajectories until they are finally resolved or reconciled by an intermediary third term. For example, the opposition between sin and God's holiness may be overcome through the mediation of redemption, or the opposition between order and chaos may be overcome through structured change.[91]

Himself an eminent sociologist of religion (which is the main disciplinary approach to the study of Japanese religions), Yanagawa found that "what makes a matsuri a matsuri" is its sensations. Others had already noted the jarring contrast of the festival's two radical aspects: its extreme solemnity and formality alongside its coarse; even obscene informality. The festival brought together respected order and "impropriety or disruption of order." American anthropologist Victor Turner had analyzed the festival as an "anti-structure"—a completely different structure than the normal world. For example, even the most funda- mental structure of the relationship between teacher and student could be reversed during the time of festival. Further, men and women might swap clothes and roles. Still, when Yanagawa added all these observations about festivals together, he concluded: "There is something else involved." He found support in a foreign scholar's report:

> ... I [William Currie] don't have any trouble recalling the combination of wonder and exhilaration I experienced that day, because the same feeling has been repeated many times during the last fifteen years.
>
> Carnivals and street fairs were not new to me, nor were outdoor religious festivals and processions. But the mixture of the sacred and the profane, the solemn and the earthy, rich symbolism and gaudy hucksterism—this was something I had not experienced before.
>
> ... Recently I attended the Night Festival at Chichibu, on the outskirts of Tokyo, one of the most colorful matsuri in all of Japan. All the elements were there that make the matsuri an exciting event: expectant crowds of people gradually becoming more and more involved in the action; the ceaseless rhythm of drums and jingling, bell-like instruments; the wild procession of *mikoshi*, or "temporary dwelling places of the gods," weaving in and out through the crowds.[92]

Currie viewed the festival from a structuralist perspective and concluded that it was a "mixture of the sacred and profane"—a classic dualism. Although Yanagawa had no interest in this type of analysis, let me interject one correction: This is *not* classic dualism; the matsuri is a unity that juxtaposes sacred and profane, proper and improper, acceptable and shocking—but leaves each element with its full power. There is no overcoming chaos or evil as there is in many other mythologies. However, even this has been said before.[93]

Yanagawa turned away from philosophizing about the event to its actual experience. Currie had described the festival as visual ("the most colorful"), "exciting", auditory ("ceaseless rhythm of drums"), with participants "weaving in and out." Here we find the "'sensory side' of matsuri," which takes the stimulation of the five senses seriously. Yanagawa's own description noted:

. . . its color, or sounds, or the pain of bearing the mikoshi (portable shrine) thus become problems of hearing, or sight, or touch, or again in the case of the foods typically consumed at the festivals, the "taste" of matsuri. When I [Yanagawa] have my students write reports of matsuri, they often say they recall the odor of acetylene gas, thus bringing in the sense of smell as well.

. . . a matsuri involves taking the conscious states received through the senses, namely sensual experience, and indulging, or using it to the greatest possible limits, without begrudging or restricting it in any way.

. . . then we have here the "ecstasy" of matsuri . . . the feeling that the people have somehow been reborn, or that they have touched something extremely fresh and new. And the conscious experiences that occur here all occurred as the result of sensations.[94]

Yanagawa has abandoned the safety of his own discipline and attempted an analysis of religious experience centered in the five senses—what we have previously called action-centered religious experience.[95] He clearly highlighted an altered state of consciousness, ecstasy, in which time returns to the beginning (as in rebirth) and one's life is made fresh and new. Yanagawa rejected not only literalism but symbolic analysis as well.[96] Here is Yanagawa's description of festival as sensation:

. . . certain states of consciousness occur from people's physiological condition, such as the musical rhythm in the matsuri, or the noise, or again the flags of various colors, the Chinese lanterns and costumes, the food, the mikoshi, the smells, or again the sense of balance and the motor activities accompanying it, and the sensations arising from the internal organs. All of these things are exploited to the fullest within the festival. Or on the contrary, in the case of fasting, the consumption of foods may be restricted to the extreme, so that festivals may involve both the aspects of dietary restriction and of gorging on unlimited quantities of food.

... the act of carrying the mikoshi, feeling the weight of it, calls up in us through our tactile sense a certain state of consciousness. The same can be said for the noise, or for the power of the alcohol in the *sake* that people drink, and if such things are called merely a symbol of symbols, or when all the things that appear within the matsuri are relegated merely to various combinations of symbols, the aspect of matsuri as sensation is, so to speak, discarded.[97]

Professor Yanagawa did not find the essence of what makes a festival a festival (*seinaru kanjô* or the feeling of the holy) in the studies of matsuri symbolism (of colors, darkness, and so forth), even though it had become a trend in religious studies. Despite his acknowledgment that he did not have a proper method or approach for this discovery, Yanagawa linked matsuri's central experience to the five senses.

Yanagawa also noted that bodily movement is related to sensate experience, and that the festival induced "ecstasy" (a standing outside of ordinary time). A line from another study of matsuri punctuates the finding that matsuri involves ecstatic experience: "When carrying the mikoshi [portable shrine] with an empty mind (*mushin*), a person enters [a] state akin to a religious ecstasy."[98]

It is to this seeming paradox that we now turn—something "akin to a religious ecstasy" found juxtaposed with the wild and seemingly profane character of matsuri. Another researcher who noted this polarity of dignified and vulgar chose to call the latter "sacred transgression."

When Japanese matsuri are considered from the standpoint of the committed believer, namely the position that such festivals represent solemn divine rites, there are numerous areas that simply defy explanation. On the one hand are highly dignified rites of seclusion and purification, tedious rites in which one's emotions and responses are trained and focused through bodily actions and behavior of the most restrained and solemn kind. On the other hand, there is also generally an expectation of a thorough liberation of mind and body, a destruction of the existing order. Festival days involve a kind of public license for the casting away of everyday restraints and for the kind of behavior that in normal common sense would be disdainfully dismissed as vulgar.[99]

Sacred transgression (*seihan*) is not a new phenomenon. There is evidence of it in Japan's first collection of poems. A "long poem" (*chôka*) in the ninth book of the *Manyôshû* links sacred space, festival, and a lapse of the normal moral order:

> On Mount Tsukuba where eagles dwell
> By the founts of Mohakitsu,
> Maidens and men, in troops assembling,
> Hold a *kagai*, vying in poetry;
> I will seek company with others' wives,
> Let others woo my own;
> The gods that dominate this mountain
> Have allowed such freedom since of old;
> This day regard us not
> With reproachful eyes,
> Nor say a word of blame.[100]

Professor Minoru Sonoda remembered his childhood experience of festivals as "a time of unease," "rowdiness," "unrestrained uproar," "wild and vulgar," "outlandish behavior," "crazed celebrations."[101] The chaotic polarity of matsuri is known as *matsuri sawagi* (festival uproar), while its solemn pole is referred to as *shukusai* (festival). Sonoda focuses on the profane or "carnival" side of matsuri.

While the solemn aspects of festival (shukusai) take place both during the day and at night, the sacred transgressions (matsuri sawagi) could hardly be allowed to see the light of day. It is at night that the human spirit changes to its rough side (*aratama*), and the prohibitions of normal time are suspended. (Shinto teaches four aspects of the spirit or soul [tama]: rough, refined, creative, and mysterious. Perhaps it is during an experience of sacred time that one learns firsthand about the fourfold soul.)

I conclude this section with a summary of a festival. Since we did not consider the rough and wild polarity of the sacred in our study of sacred action (rituals), and only very slightly in the sacred stories (myths), we will join the festival at night as it enters its chaotic state.

The priest has held a solemn procession and has prayed for the success of the night's celebration and the safety of all participants and observers. Suddenly the throng explodes into unrestrained noise and seemingly dangerous behaviors. All the pent-up energies of Japan's fairly rigid social structure are about to be released. But all is not as it seems. Copying the orderliness of daytime, there have been many rehearsals for this night of chaos, even contracts and vows to follow the lead of the ceremonial leader. But soon there would be danger—not just imagined, since histories record near riots and past injuries as young men overturned a hierarchy based on seniority and status. Their power propels the wild energies of the night.

Our "typical" last night of the festival pits ten teams of a hundred youths each against each other. The teams carry festival floats with eight drummers aboard. Disruptors carrying what is effectively a battering ram with a drum add to the fray. This is the third night of suspended time (following the ancient schedule of the rice harvest when everyone could be freed from their ordinary schedule). Some might see this as the end of a mating ritual in which young men compete with "immoderate braggadocio" before and for young village women. Without much sleep and already beyond normal limits of alcohol consumption, modesty vanishes. The young men are clad only in belly and head bands (the festival is referred to by local merchants advertising for tourists as a "naked festival"). Each float has its own drummers and chant, the hundred bearers moving or dancing, colliding forcefully with other floats at village intersections. Curses and vulgarities erupt in drunken quarrels and aggressive behavior. Fatigue and cold bring frequent mishaps with some being trampled beneath a float and its hundred surging bodies. Gangs of a dozen or so disruptors attempt to charge through the float carriers and destroy the main drum with their battering ram. Danger, fear, pain, competition, and aggression abound. Ridicule comes from competitors and observers as all boundaries blur with drink and excitement; primal behavior erases daytime restraints. The drumming and dancing lead to a new intoxication—a hypnotic state of trance or "possession" in an "eternal timelessness." In this darkened time, the participants are quite "other" than themselves. Observers get sucked into the chaos, are affected by the bombardment of the senses, are drawn into the unexpected dangers and risks, and are also "possessed" by the sheer power and energy of the spectacle. Spectators alternately flee and are struck by the naked demon-dancers. The sounds of women screaming, children sobbing, and tourists shouting testify to the pandemonium and anarchy of the night. "It's scary." "I didn't expect such violence from this docile village." "It wasn't as exciting as last year." Everyone has a different account of matsuri sawagi (festival uproar).

When the forces of chaos and disruption have been exhausted, the rituals of order and decency slowly reappear. Participants are feasted in village homes and respect, good manners, and polite behavior returns. Harmony and order return to this peaceful loving village.

It is only in a shrine's major matsuri that the full juxtaposition of chaos and harmony can be experienced. Minor festivals have less of the wild and rough polarity of the sacred. In fact, the disruptive and profane may only appear in moments of subtle laughter and humor. Because the chaotic and unstructured character of sacred time is dangerous, rituals may be used to routinize sacred time and make it safe, rather than being used to propel one out of ordinary time.

Paradoxically, while the purpose of matsuri is to experience the sacred, the unresolved tension between the wild and the solemn makes sacred time barely "experience-able."

SCHEDULING SACRED TIME

The first observation I will make about scheduling sacred time in Japan is that it is still linked to rice and its cultivation. The cycles of agricultural times are reflected in the Shinto ritual calendar. Even the New Year marks a special occasion in the life cycle of rice.

My second observation is that it is difficult to schedule sacred time, which is a "time out of time," into our busy calendars. This worked much better in the agricultural village than it does in the modern city. At one time, Japan's farmers lived in and around rice production. There were periods of necessary labor interspersed with brief periods that could be placed outside of ordinary time. The latter were times of festival and celebration. Everyone could participate; all ordinary work stopped. Such a demarcation of time is no longer possible in modern city life, where services as well as medical care (and a myriad of other modern activities) must go on nonstop. Festivals that cannot preserve this feature of a time out of time turn into a tourist event—an activity that bears little resemblance to sacred time. There is just no time for the entire community to come together and celebrate for several days or a week as was done in the past in rural Japan. Festivals have been shortened, the calendar adjusted so that the central event can fall on a weekend, and the character of the celebration itself may have been drastically modified to meet modern preferences. Even in Japan, it is hard to find an authentic "folk festival." More and more, festivals have lost their local flavor and are tailored to draw the most tourists and earn the most money. Thus, mythological time has been gobbled up by historical and commercial time. (Some argue that "real festivals" will soon disappear because modern life just does not support a "time out of the ordinary.")

Festivals (matsuri) vary from shrine to shrine. This variety is also rapidly disappearing, but for so long as it survives it is a reminder of the tension between a unified Shinto tradition and the many independent shrine traditions. We will look at the most important festivals at Tsubaki Grand Shrine, where I have been a visitor twenty-six times. Those who are interested in learning what happens in a different locale should consult John Nelson's wonderful sociological study of another shrine's festival year.[102]

The calendar year (*nen-chu-gyo-ji*, literally "year-round-discipline-rituals") refers to the Shinto annual calendar of events. From the perspective of Shrine Shinto and the priest who will officiate at the festivals, these rituals make up the cycle of activities that occupy the priests of the shrine from one year to the next.

Oshôgatsu—New Year [103]

The end of the old year and the beginning of the New Year are very important times in Japan. From the perspective of mythic time or sacred time, New Year is the time when the cycle of life is renewed.

Toward the end of the old year, people gather for *bonenkai*, year-end parties at which the irritations, frustrations, and any misfortunes of the past year are symbolically washed away—and forgotten—in the sake drunk on these occasions. After the New Year has been ceremonially ushered in, people hold *shinenkai* or New Year parties, toasting the New Year, expressing their hopes and expectations for the year to come, wishing each other well, and anticipating the good things to be.

About a month before the New Year, at the beginning of December, people traditionally put up an "entrance pine" (*kadomatsu*) in front of their home. A combination of standing bamboo and pine branches, the kadomatsu welcomes the kami whose goodwill and blessings are being sought. In today's cities, the entrance pine usually goes up the last week of December on either side of the doorways to houses, hotels, offices, bars, and even bath houses. The shortened New Year celebration is blamed on the pressures of business life. In the rural areas, where the whole celebration was based on the patterns of a rice culture, New Year's festivities used to last until January 15 (*koshogatsu*, literally "Little New Year"), and could continue even beyond that into February.

Other New Year preparations include a ceremonial house cleaning (*susuharai*) followed by the preparation of traditional cold dishes called *osechi-ryori* and *motchitsuki*, rice cake. (The reason that food was served cold was to relieve housewives of the task of cooking for the opening three days of the New Year.) The ideal of finishing the food preparation ahead of time is not so easy to accomplish today, given the increase in the number of visitors coming and going during this holiday. The closing event of the old year is eating a final plate of Japanese noodles (*toshi-koshi-soba*).

On New Year's Eve, a family will either visit the local shrine just after midnight or await the New Year at home. If they remain at home, a family will clap their hands in front of the kamidana (the shelf on which a miniature shrine is placed) and make offerings to the kami as the New Year arrives. Some people go out to watch the first sunrise of the year (*hatsu-hi-node*), while others simply go to a shrine the first two or three days of the year (*hatsumôde*). People exchange New Year's visits (*nenga*) and cards (*nengajo*).

Children receive money (*otoshidama*) for the New Year, while adults involve themselves in a whole range of traditional New Year activities, such as ladies in *kimono* playing a kind of badminton, men playing card and dice games and, in some rural areas, costumed men called *namahage* visiting homes to see if the young are behaving well.

Seijin-no-hi—January 15

Seijin-no-hi is coming-of-age day—in Japan one comes of age on one's twentieth birthday. Shinto celebrates decisive moments in the life cycle. Local town halls give presents to the year's new twenty-year-olds. Girls will often dress in *kimono* for picture-taking. This was also the traditional time for marriage. At twenty, one is recognized as a full member of society. This event is marked with a visit to the shrine for a blessing from the kami, and a celebration of one's new status.

Setsubun—February 3

Setsubun-no-hi is celebrated with the *Setsubun* festival (matsuri). Setsubun means the day before the official beginning of spring.

According to the old calendar, it marks the end of winter. The "old year" is brought to an end by bean throwing, which takes place both at home and at the local shrine. The purpose of the bean throwing is to expel bad fortune and invoke good fortune. At Tsubaki, priests dress in classic costume and shrine members join in a procession for purification. Then, from a great platform raised in front of the shrine sanctuary (haiden), priests and dignitaries—most often *sumo* champions—throw packets of beans for members and visitors to catch. The chief priest (*Guji*) of the shrine shoots an arrow to break the power of misfortune. Then the crowd processes to the ceremony.

Toshi-goi-no-matsuri—February 21

Toshi-goi-no-matsuri is also known as the *yakuyoke* festival. Yakuyoke refers to a talisman or omamori that is designed to ward off evil influences. The festival is linked closely to societal rites of passage and deals with the problems faced by people at particularly difficult times in their lives. One life-cycle celebration is the coming of manhood for young men at age seventeen. The parallel celebration for young women occurs at age nineteen (*genbuku*). The more dangerous or inauspicious ages (*yakudoshi*), when misfortunes are most likely, are twenty-one and thirty-three for women and forty-two for men. Such times require special purification. Later in life, both men and women celebrate *kanreki* at age sixty-one. Additional life-cycle celebrations occur at ages seventy, seventy-seven, eighty-eight, and ninety-nine. The flow of good and bad fortune is often associated with a particular physical symbol, the arrow that breaks misfortune. It is usually installed in the kamidana.

Hina-matsuri—March

Hina-matsuri, the festival of dolls, celebrates a family's daughters. The dolls are dressed in Heian-era costumes that may be very old, having been handed down from mother to daughter for generations. Traditional food, various celebrations, and a shrine visit are associated with hina-matsuri.

Shubun-sai—March 21

Shubun-sai is equinox day, a day for visiting ancestral graves. It is closely associated with Buddhism, having become part of the annual cycle of events and national holidays when Buddhism and Shinto were merged.

Haru Matsuri—End of March

Haru matsuri, the spring festival, begins toward the end of March and lasts approximately until the end of April. It marks the traditional date of completion of rice planting. Even today it is a time of praying for a successful harvest, and it is one of the major events of the year. All the priests of each shrine process in full ceremonial dress and enter the haiden for the purification rites (harai).

Koi-no-bori—May 5

Koi-no-bori is the boys' festival. Large cloth carp identify the homes where there are boys. The carp is admired because of its ability to swim against the stream and is a fitting model for youth to emulate. A common household decoration is a model of the kind of helmet worn by the ancient samurai.

Natsu-matsuri—June

Natsu-matsuri lasts for almost the entire month of June. This summer festival is celebrated during the time when the crops are in the greatest danger of being destroyed by insects or disease. Storms and floods can cause enormous damage as well. The blessing of the kami is sought at this tenuous time.

Nagoshi-no-Oharai—June 30

Nagoshi-no-Oharai is a form of purification involving walking through a circle of rope. A large sacred ring called a *chi-no-wa*, made of loosely twisted miscanthus reeds, is set up and after oharai people walk through it. It was originally intended for the purification of agricultural workers, to ward off mishaps of every kind. It is performed on June 30, one of the two great days of national purification (*Ôharae*; the other great day of national purification falls on December 31 and is called *Shiwasu-Oharai*). Nagoshi-no-Oharai completes the rites of the summer period. Today the summer festivals attract many tourists, as well as remaining popular with the local people. The large crowds reflect the fact that these festivals take place between sowing and harvesting, during a relatively slow-paced time of the year.

Aki-matsuri—September to November
The Autumn Festival, *Aki-matsuri*, takes place during the months of September to November. For many shrines, it is the main festival of the year. The community gathers to offer thanksgiving for the incoming harvest. The Autumn Festival is the sequel to the Spring Festival. October is known in Japanese as *kan-na-zuki*, the month when the kami are absent. For this reason, September was traditionally a month of strict taboos.

At Tsubaki Grand Shrine, *Rei-tai-sai* is celebrated between October 11 and 13. It is a festival associated with Sarutuhiko Okami. In the neighboring Ise Jingu, where Amaterasu Ômikami is enshrined, a festival called *Kannamae-sai* takes place in mid-October. During this festival the first fruits of the grain harvest are offered to the Deity of the Sun. Closely related to this, and held at Tsubaki Grand Shrine on November 23, is the festival known as *Niiname-sai*, a very old and important festival held once a year that, like the Kannamae-sai, has to do with the agricultural cycle. At the Ise celebration, the emperor offers the first cuttings of the harvest, just as a local village headman would do at a village shrine.

Shichi-go-san—November 15
Shichi-go-san, the festival for three-, five-, and seven-year-olds, is a national festival held around November 15. Children in classical dress are taken to shrines to seek the protection of the kami in this delicate stage of their lives.

Oshôgatsu—End of Year

After November, we come to the end of the year and the Oshôgatsu festival, and the cycle begins all over again.

CONCLUSION

Shrine Shinto's sense of sacred time is both ritualistic and liturgical. The regularity of the cycle of rice cultivation shows up everywhere. Perhaps it is not too harsh to conclude that some routinization has occurred, and the dynamic experience of sacred time has been modified by an emphasis on solemnity, symmetry, and harmony. Nature's beauty has replaced its power. Time may even be standing still.

7

Sacred Ruler

When the sun shall hide
behind the green mountains,
in the night black as the true jewels
of the moor will I come forth.

—Second Song of the Princess, the *Kojiki*

FROM CHAOS TO DIVINE ORDER

Villages, cities, monasteries, and even the royal court were struck by periods of lawlessness. They suffered the horrors and cruelties of being victimized by armed assailants. Social chaos gave birth to a longing for a divinely ordained order, one given by the ruling kami of the highest heaven, Amaterasu Ômikami. Out of the chaos of banditry, and the brutalities of war, pillage, and rape, there emerged a potent symbol that was destined to unite Japan under a single vision of life. The Japanese came to believe that life was whole and complete only when lived under the reign of Amaterasu's heirs on earth, the imperial family and its head, the Tennô, the divine ruler.[104]

The vision of a sacred ruler resides in several Japanese words: *sumera-mikoto,* tennô, *kimi,* and *mikado*. While the notion of a divine emperor has a longer history in China, Chinese terms were not adopted without change. The Chinese terms in question are *di, huang, huang di, tianzi,* and *tian huang.*

WORDS ENVISIONING A SACRED RULER

Sumera-mikoto [105] was a local or Japanese term. Japanese linguists say that *sumera* meant "dwelling or speaking" and *mikoto* meant "holy word." Nobutsuna Saigo argued that sumera meant "being clean." These ancient meanings pointed to a shamanic ruler who received the oracles of the kami, who was pure enough to be in communication with the kami. The roles of religious leader and military protector were combined in this charismatic ruler. The kanji is tennô in its Chinese pronunciation.

While Sumera-mikoto may have been the first Japanese term for emperor, there may have been an earlier term (*ôkimi* or "great lord") used for the Yamato rulers. The term used for rulers in the *Kojiki* and *Nihonshoki* is kimi.[106] There is still much philological work to be done even in this relatively well-researched area. Kimi is used in the term for imperial reign and in the title of the Japanese national anthem (*kimigayo*).

The term that was used for the divine emperor following the Imperial Restoration (1868–1945) was mikado, literally "exalted gate." Mikado was originally a term of endearment, but it came to be associated with the militarism of the two world wars and is no longer used.

SACRED RULER AND DIVINE ORDER

Originally, there was no lord or king of the heavens. In the classical Shinto myths, the kami acted as an assembly. This was true even after the Yamato imperial court promoted their goddess, Amaterasu Ômikami, to the position of principal ruler of heaven.

Sociologists use the old adage "On earth, so in heaven" to interpret how a society envisions divine governance, and then uses that idea to justify the type of government it has developed on earth. Despotic kings seem much more tolerable if a society believes that the heavens also enshrine a despot as divine ruler and potentate.

Imperial Shinto would finally ascribe fully dictatorial powers to Japan's earthly ruler, while the reality was far from that. Amaterasu, the Sun Goddess, became more powerful in the imperial ideology, almost absolute in her power over heaven and earth. But the Japanese emperor on earth was only a thin disguise for an imperial state of bureaucrats, military leaders, and industrialists. It was the militaristic state that was absolute—with the divine right to rule both its people and the world as it alone saw fit. Imperial or State Shinto failed utterly to provide an ethical corrective to the abuse of power by these military leaders. However, State Shinto and Imperial Japan can be used as a perfect example to illustrate the adage "On earth, so in heaven."

Shrine Shinto faces an ethical crisis involving both vision and leadership. Even though it has been separated from government and governmental control for approximately a half century, Shrine Shinto still envisions itself as integral to the governing of Japan according to the divine order as laid down in the Japanese Classics. It has yet to find a new way to exercise cultural and social leadership. Its vision remains in the past, copying ancient myths, and its leadership spends its time attempting to conserve a past that is no more. Not surprisingly, its evaluation of society and culture remain consistently negative and almost reactionary. Sectarian Shinto groups are far more in tune with democracy and far more open to new cultural possibilities, even though their members may come from classes with less power and wealth.

In traditional Japan, persons of noble rank were never addressed by their given name. Today, this convention still applies in the case of the imperial family. While in English we might refer to the current emperor as Akihito or Emperor Akihito, someone from Japan would refer to him indirectly as Tennô Heika (literally "His Majesty the Emperor") or less often as Kinjô Tennô. Past emperors are referred to by the name of their era (e.g., "Meiji," "Shôwa," or "Heisei" plus "Tennô"), or by their posthumous name. Emperor Hirohito is now referred to as Shôwa Tennô. His Imperial Majesty Emperor Akihito has been on the throne since his father Hirohito died in 1989. His era is Heisei, so the year 2004 on the Gregorian calendar is Heisei 15 (this is an example of the imperial chronology that some wish to make official again).

SOME CHINESE TERMS AND CONCEPTS

A Chinese character for king or emperor was huang in pinyin. There was the Daoist legend of the three god-kings (heavenly, earthly, human). Another character for ruler or emperor was di in pinyin. There were five emperors who were morally perfect, according to Daoist legend. But the principal concept in China was that the ruler was divine through his adoption by Heaven (*tian* in pinyin). The emperor of China was the "son of Heaven" or *tianzi* and consequently divine (*tian huang*, heavenly emperor). The emperor's adoption was based on merit and had to be maintained through the proper exercise of office. This meant that new dynastic lineages could supersede previous ones if it was deemed that they were chosen by Heaven. This was not the case in Japan, however, where any qualification other than birth was rejected. There was only one Japanese lineage, that of the Yamato, known as the Tennô line. They were to be divine rulers forever.

SHINTO VISIONS OF THE SACRED RULER

All forms of Shinto share the belief that the ruler of Japan, the land of the kami, is divine. Each of the different types of Shinto has its own vision of the divine ruler but the symbol is shared by all of them.

Shamanic Shinto

Shamanic religion originated long before recorded history and long before Japan borrowed the Chinese writing system. It certainly predates imperial efforts to unify religion and government. The shamans and shamanesses communed with the spirits, became possessed, and gave guidance in oracles about all of life's concerns—crops, health, war, pestilence, and death. Tragically, very little of these early practices has survived.[107] I had the good fortune to learn from a Shinto shamanness, Ikuko Osumi[108]—but that world of shamanic healers is rapidly disappearing.[109]

As Max Weber so brilliantly demonstrated in his studies,[110] shamanic power—independent of worldly and military power— is a rival to even the most elementary forms of government. Even after power and privilege are consolidated in a secular ruler, a shaman (one who communicates with the gods) or a prophet (one whose words can indict even kings) can delegitimate the secular leader's claim of a divine right to rule. (Weber and the sociology of religion have dominated religious studies in Japan.)

At the very moment at which Japan appears on the stage of history (by appearing in the records of China and Korea), shamans are involved in the rule of its emerging royal states. In such a situation, if the religious function dominates a theocracy is formed; but if secular/military rule dominates, then religion is used to bolster the interests of the institutions of government. Weber called the latter scenario *caesaro-papism*, a term intended to indicate that the primary interest of this form of government would be power and privilege, not religion. At this point, we are ready to describe the first major ancient unifier of these two competing powers (religion and rule): Himiko, queen of Wa.

Himiko is mentioned in Chinese records as the shaman-queen of the Japanese kingdom of Wa (its capital was Yamatai). Indeed, Japan was at first called the Queenly Kingdom. The Chinese Han dynasty had split into three kingdoms, one of which was Wei. Wei sent a military expedition in the 230s and established its rule of Manchuria and Korea. The Wei then sought friendly relations with the Japanese kingdom of Wa, probably on the island of Kyushu. Queen Himiko and the Wei emperor exchanged several delegations. The written records of the Chinese observers of this state ruled by a shaman-queen are quite extensive.[111]

Queen Himiko was not married and preferred seclusion in her well-fortified palace to attendance at functions of state. She ruled through her brother, receiving revelations from the kami in states of possession. She was attended by a thousand female servants. Some scholars think she did not unite religion and rule in her own person but rather started the tendency in Japan for dual rule—one ruler who was a symbol and whose power was primarily religious, and another ruler—the actual power-holder—who was secular. Perhaps the strongest counter argument to this view comes from Moriyuki Abukuma.[112] Abukuma appears to have found the first usage of the term sumera-mikoto (or tennô when expressed with Chinese characters and a Sino-Japanese pronunciation).[113] Recall that the original meaning of sumera-mikoto was "dwelling or speaking the holy word [of the kami]," and that the meaning of the term also involved "being clean." Himiko led in the worship of a sun goddess, using bronze mirrors in the rituals.[114] When commanded to do so by the gods (*kotomuke*), Himiko sent her army to pacify *araburu-kami*, the wild "men's house" gangs that disturbed the land. The Chinese records state that Himiko unified twenty-eight countries, indicating that her military exploits were quite successful.

None of the above is disputed by scholars, as it derives from the records of the Chinese observers who visited her kingdom. Abukuma points to *Nihonshoki* references to a Princess Yamato-toto-momoso-hime, which he thinks is the Japanese name of Queen Himiko. In this instance, she is only made a princess, but an alternative viewpoint (and remember that this is the style of the *Nihonshoki*) declares Himiko (now a male) to be emperor (sumera-mikoto) and founder of the nation (*hatsu-kuni-shirasu*).[115] When Queen Himiko of the Chinese records died, "a mound 145 meters in diameter was made for her tomb, and more than 100 slaves were buried with her."[116] A man, perhaps one of her generals, succeeded her but could not quiet the disorder. Next, a thirteen-year-old girl, perhaps another shamaness-queen, came to power. The Chinese record of their contact with the Wa ends at this point.

Shamanic Shinto would be routinized, ritualized, and would eventually evolve into Shrine Shinto. Its vision of the priest-emperor would be further developed in Sectarian Shinto and the renewal of the emperor's divine spirit (see below).

Imperial Shinto

"Imperial Household Shinto" is the modern term; it reflects the 1945 defeat of Japan in World War II and postwar terminology. From the time of the early Yamato rulers, Japanese imperial religion utilized all the religions found in Japan (shamanism, Shinto, Buddhism, Confucianism, Daoism, and lesser mainland and Japanese indigenous religions). The Yamato selected portions of these religious traditions and modified them in order to construct their ideology of imperial rule. For example, they modified the Confucian vision of a divine ruler. In the Chinese version, the ruler was chosen by Heaven (*tian, t'ien*)[117] and given the mandate (*ming*) to rule. A Chinese imperial dynasty would remain "chosen" as long as it followed the proper way (*dao/tao*) or order (*li*) of Heaven. However, the mandate to rule could be withdrawn, and it was believed that a dynasty would fall if it ceased to follow Heaven's way (*tian-dao*). Japanese scholars thought the Chinese version of divine rule sounded like an invitation to rebellion, so they "purified" the concept. They adopted the idea that the emperor was "son of God," but took it more literally. They disposed of the historical fact that other families or clans had ruled kingdoms in Japan before the Yamato, and connected their dynasty directly to the heavenly ruler, the head of the kami.

We recall that in the *Kojiki* and the *Nihonshoki*, the Izumo were characterized as surrendering their rule of earth to Amaterasu's grandson and his heirs. The Yamato notion of the "heavenly emperor" does not even acknowledge this prior rule. It simply begins civilization with the coming of the first Yamato ruler. He begins the rice culture and, with it, Amaterasu's proper order of the earth. Susanoo, Amaterasu's brother and the kami worshipped by the Izumo, was stigmatized and reduced to a mixture of star god, storm god, and god of the sea/land.

Another claimant for ruler of earth was Sarutahiko Okami, chief of earthly kami.[118] He was married to Uzume, kami of dance, entertainment, and literature. Once again, Sarutahiko's legendary status as the pioneer kami, the discoverer of the Japanese archipelago, and the ruler of earth was simply ignored by the Yamato.

The clan deity of the Yamato was Amaterasu Ômikami. Their imperial texts, the *Kojiki* and the *Nihonshoki*, raised their goddess to supremacy over all the other kami—both heavenly and earthly. The only thing that kept this mythological coup from defining more of Japanese history than it did in fact define was the fact that this early form of State Shinto was downplayed by the Nara emperors, who chose Buddhism rather than Shinto as their state religion. Shinto's vision of imperial descent from the Sun Goddess, and her proclamation that one imperial family would rule forever, was nonetheless a wonderful legitimizing and stabilizing factor for Japan's rulers. The Yamato vision would become central in the great Meiji Restoration of imperial rule in the nineteenth century, and it would be fundamental in creating State Shinto (*Kokugaku* Shinto).

Daoism and the Chinese philosophies (*yin-yang* and the five-elements) played a lesser role in defining the notion of divine imperial rule. For most of Japanese history, the main ideology supporting the notion of a divine imperial ruler would be Buddhist. The specific type of Buddhism used was an esoteric form derived from the Shingon and Tendai schools. It viewed the ruler as a manifestation of the cosmic Buddha

Daiinichi (the so-called Sun Buddha), or more simply as a living boddhisattva (a Buddha-to-be). Either way, this Buddhist ideology covered the emperor in divinity and made the imperial office one of the most stable forms of government devised by any culture. Furthermore, these Buddhist views complemented both the Confucian view of the ruler as "son of Heaven" and the Shinto view of the ruler as divine descendant.

The idea that the emperor was a manifestation of the Sun Buddha worked perfectly with the Shinto notion of descent from Amaterasu, the Sun Goddess. In fact, the conception of Amaterasu as Sun Goddess may be largely a Buddhist idea. The original portrayal of Amaterasu in the *Kojiki* names her as Amaterasu-o-mi-kami, the Heaven-Shining-Great-August-kami. The *Kojiki* does not objectify the sun as a kami, nor does it personify the kami-ness of the sun as a goddess. If kami was originally conceived of as "divine immanent power" or "awesome manifestation," (see chapter two), then this imperial notion of Amaterasu as Sun Goddess is more indebted to Buddhism than it is to early Shinto. Buddhist skill-in-teaching (*upaya*) allows the teaching of "relative truth" or "illusions" to those not capable of grasping the full Buddhist teaching, the *dharma*. This allowed Buddhists to both affirm the emperor as descendant of Amaterasu Ômikami (thereby holding the ruler to a Buddhist standard of righteousness), and deny that this notion had any ultimate validity for those who understood the entire Buddhist truth. For centuries no Buddhist monk would bow to any earthly ruler—but that finally changed in Japan.

Imperial Shinto would transmute in the nineteenth century into State Shinto. After World War II, it became known as Imperial Household Shinto.

"For example, the so-called Imperial Household Shinto, that is, the religious rites performed at the three shrines within the imperial palace, continues as ever before, except that it is now supposed to be the private affair of the imperial family. Moreover, the transition from State Shinto to Shrine Shinto did not affect Shinto rites practiced in individual homes. Devout adherents of Shinto still perform their daily ablutions and pay homage at the family shrine as they have always done, and visit their tutelary shrines on special occasions."[119]

We note in closing this section that Imperial Shinto's view of the Sacred Ruler would come as close to an orthodox belief as Shinto would ever have.

State Shinto

The emperor was "restored" as divine ruler of the state in 1868, ushering in the Meiji Era (1868–1912). The political system changed from rule by the shogun[120] to rule in the name of the emperor and according to his divine will by an oligarchy of bureaucrats. This was known as "the Meiji Restoration." Actual rule never passed into the hands of the divine ruler; he was kept busy with ever more rituals that combined religion and state. Buddhism was replaced as the state religion by Shinto. After a short time, however, Shinto was redefined as patriotism (therefore not a religion), so that every Japanese person could be forced to practice the new state ideology. This new state ideology is what we are calling State Shinto. In Japan it was called Kokugaku ("national learning"), or, more properly, *Kokutai* ("national essence"). Kokutai imposed the following six elements on the Japanese people: (1) belief that the emperor was "sacred and inviolable"; (2) worship of the spirits of the imperial ancestors, as well as worship of imperial decrees; (3) unquestioning acceptance of ancient myths and their chauvinistic [*sic*.] interpretation in modern works like the nationalistic textbook *Kokutai no Hongi*; (4) observance of national holidays, which focused on the glorification of the imperial line; (5) worship of kami at shrines and in the home; and (6) financial support of local shrines and festivals.[121]

Commodore Perry's humiliation of the shogunate in 1853 was a defining moment in Japanese history. Out of the turmoil arose a national consciousness—"Japaneseness."[122] A feeling of national inferiority and humiliation paradoxically gave rise to the realization that to be Japanese meant to be part of a nation that was the land of the kami, and which was led by a ruler who was a descendant of the greatest kami of them all, Amaterasu, the Sun Goddess. To be Japanese entailed being part of a mission foretold in the Classics—to pacify the land, to purify it, to bring order (harmony) and civilization to it. The Classics described warrior emperors who not only subdued the wild elements in the Japanese islands, but conquered other kingdoms as well (especially the kingdoms of Korea).

Japan had faced foreign evil before, in the invasion of the Mongolian hordes in 1274. During that time a "divine wind" (*kamikaze*) saved Japan from sure disaster. If only Japan had a sacred ruler, people reasoned, it could arise and assume its rightful place among the modern nations. And, it could begin to establish its rule over the nations of Asia, as had been foretold in the *Kojiki*. (The belief that Japan was destined to rule Asia was based on a dubious interpretation of a single verse, but that does not change the fact that most Japanese of this period firmly believed in it).

As Western nations forced open the ports of Japan and wrote unequal treaties, the power and legitimacy of the shogunate appeared null and void. A restoration movement swept aside the last shogun and promised that Japan would once again be ruled by a descendant of Amaterasu. But what kind of rulership would this restoration achieve? First, it would be hereditary. Almost no one doubted that the emperor had a special (divine) birth, or the accuracy of the Classics' representation of the imperial family as a single lineage of divine rulers. Second, it would be sacerdotal—the emperor was the high priest of the Goddess Amaterasu and the nation. The rituals would again be performed in the imperial shrines of the nation—mainly Ise Grand Shrine, but others as well. With the restoration of the emperor came the disestablishment of Buddhism as the state religion and the establishment of Shinto. Third, it would be expansionary. Japan sent an expeditionary force to Formosa (now Taiwan) in 1874. The Sino-Japanese War (1894–1895) brought the acquisition of Taiwan. Japan joined the Western colonial powers in putting down the so-called Boxer Rebellion in China. Japan defeated Russia in the Russo-Japanese War of 1904–1905. In 1910, Japan annexed Korea. During World War I, Japan joined the Allies and succeeded in attaining most of her goals at the Versailles Conference. The fact that actual rulership was consolidated in a military-industrial alliance brought Japan into further conflicts across Asia. Beginning in 1937, there would be full-scale war in China, clashes with the Soviet Union in 1938 and 1939, and finally joining of the Tripartite Pact with Italy and Germany in 1940.

There was much controversy about the role of Emperor Hirohito during World War II. Was he a ceremonial ruler like his immediate predecessors, or was he commander-in-chief of the nation and high priest of the state religion? United States General Douglas MacArthur sided with those who believed the emperor should be left in place, to counter the threat of Japan becoming a Communist state. The emperor would be forced to renounce his claim to divinity and become merely a "symbol of the nation."

"The disestablishment of State Shinto in 1945 by means of the Shinto Directive of the occupation authorities opened a new page in the history of Shinto. Government subsidy of Shinto establishments was discontinued, and the farmlands belonging to the shrines were lost under the land reform program."[123]

Shrine Shinto

Scholars have analyzed Shinto's nineteenth century turn toward militarism and imperialism in various ways. Some consider it a sudden departure from the genuinely spiritual nature of Shinto. Others have argued that all major religions (as we know them today) are the result of the political institutionalization of spiritual practices—that is simply what we mean by calling something a religion. Certainly one strand of Shrine Shinto was manipulated by the state and placed in the service of a drive toward political unification and legitimization. As we have continually noted, however, the local character of Shrine Shinto has never been lost—it was continuously preserved in local sacred stories and festivals. However, Shrine Shinto never developed an alternative view of the relationship between Shinto and the state. It appeared willing to accept State Shinto's view of the sacred ruler and of seisai itchi, the unification of worship and government.

Religious or Sectarian Shinto

Sectarian Shinto includes thirteen Shinto denominations (or sects as they are called in Japan) that were founded by individuals in the nineteenth century. Japanese New Religions, many of them founded after World War II, are also included in Sectarian Shinto. Sectarian Shinto is the small portion of Shinto that was just too religious to be defined as state ideology or Japanese patriotism (Kokugaku).

The world of the Japanese New Religions and the thirteen Shinto denominations can be quite bewildering. Even now, after having visited many of their headquarters and talked with their representatives, I am still amazed that there are so many differences. What I want to do is simplify all of these differences around two themes: a true divine ruler and a purified people. I will summarize an exciting chapter by Michihito Tsushima in a book on the *New Religions*.[124] He has focused on an obscure group, Shinsei Ryûjinkai, and its founder, Yûtarô Yano (1881–1938).

Yano began life as a Buddhist but went through some of the revival or restoration Shinto groups of the early twentieth century. He died in prison in 1938 (or was killed there by the Japanese High Police). Yano was charged with the crime of disrespect to the emperor and to Ise Grand Shrine. The bill of indictment read:

> In flagrant disregard for the classics of Japanese history, this group teaches the absurd notion that, in addition to the sole con-sanguineous genealogy of historical emperors and empresses, there is another, so-called spirit geneology, and that some of the historical line of emperors and empresses actually belong to a spirit genealogy of evil deities and spirits of foreign origin, in this way defaming the imperial dignity.

They further raise dreadful heresies regarding the divine body (goshintai) kept at the Grand Shrine of Ise and also promote rash and blind theories about the three divine treasures, damaging the prestige of the Grand Shrine, while otherwise using the pretext of divine revelations to spread inflammatory and disrespectful teachings, thus showing disrespect to the emperor and the Grand Shrine.[125]

Yano, like many other religious leaders who lived during the period of State Shinto, was prosecuted for teaching views that were not consistent with the state religion, Kokutai or national essence. His studies of the Japanese Classics were a bit bizarre by modern standards. He practiced spiritual disciplines that allowed him to go into trance. While in trance, he would receive answers to questions (either by automatic writing or through oracles) that went beyond the information included in the Classics. (Actually, Yano's wife was more talented at receiving the voices of the kami—"channeling"—than he was.)

Yano posed questions that reflected a modern Japanese set of concerns. For example, how could the versions of creation found in the *Kojiki* and the *Nihonshoki* be complete if Japan alone was mentioned? How did the other nations come into being? What is the relationship of the divine ruler[126] to the other nations? And was there no standard for divinity in human emperors? In other words, when the living emperor no longer acted in the way that emperors acted during the age of the gods (kamiyo) was he still divine? Or, asking the same question in yet another way, did he still have the divine spirit (mitama)?

Yano, who had been a decorated naval officer, was on the verge of what would be considered treason. The answers that he received to his questions echoed those of other groups that he had visited. One such group had produced a document with a writing system that purportedly derived from the age of the gods. This was known as the Takeuchi Document (*Takeuchi monjo*). It extended the imperial line back further than the Classics, accounted for the creation of other nations, and asserted the supremacy of the divine ruler of Japan over all other nations and peoples. Yano's shamanic revelations agreed with the Takeuchi history and added another history of even greater importance: a spirit history of the life of the gods (kami) that served as the master plan of what happened on earth. The events of this world reflected what was happening in the divine world.

Yano's revelations were an implicit criticism of the living emperor and most emperors before him—they simply had not fulfilled the divine plan. They were supposed to set up a rule of order (harmony: wa) and purity (harai—another sign of true divinity), not just for Japan but for all of the world. Yano and his group (Shinsei Ryûjinkai) were supposed to purify themselves and then convince the emperor of his need for purification and the renewal of his divine spirit (mitama). His divinity would be renewed and he would be able to lead Japan and the world to peace and prosperity. The emperor would have as his advisors and administrators the elite members of Shinsei Ryûjinkai.

Whether one smiles at such political naiveté or not, this vision of divine rule and the Japanese mission spoke deeply to a number of important people during these crisis years in Japan. It addressed some of the very same emotions that the military state was exploiting: the desire for a divine ruler, a longing for a national mission or destiny, and hope for peace and prosperity. Japan sought renewed strength and courage to face the evil forces that sought their own selfish desires and profits. "Evil" was equated with "foreign." Foreign influences (evil kami) had brought an end to the harmony of the Kami-yo (divine age), and in the modern period foreign influences (China, the United States, and Western colonial powers) were once again threatening Japan's destiny.

The Japanese military regime shared some of Yano's ideas, at least to a point. They, too, sought to fulfill the divine mission and destiny of Japan to rule the world. They, too, preached that it would take discipline to change Japan and the world. (Yano equated discipline with purification, but the military thought of it as *Bushidô*, the code of loyalty and obedience to duty.)

However, totalitarianism does not allow independent thought, action, or criticism. Yano's independent reading of the Japanese Classics did not support the ideology of the state. Rather, it led him to criticize the emperor. Yano claimed that the emperor was not a living kami, but rather an emperor whose spirit was no longer divine. (Remember that he was charged with defaming the imperial dignity.) He questioned the continuous bloodline genealogy of the imperial house, even stating that some of the emperors were not to be counted in this lineage because they had lived in such a despicable way. He also contended that there was foreign blood in the royal bloodline!

There could be only one state-authorized form of Shinto, and that was the one taught in the name of the Grand Shrine (Ise). Yano had cast doubt on the symbols of divine rule enshrined there. State Shinto could not allow that to happen. Ise Shinto had become the state-dictated ideology of an imperialism and militarism gone mad. Yano would die for his vision and Shinsei Ryûjinkai would disappear without a trace.

All religious or sectarian Shinto groups whose teachings differed from the state-dictated ideology were persecuted and some were exterminated. The term "State Shinto" is never used in Japan today because it is a reminder of the enormous failure of the state ideology and its corrupted vision of the sacred ruler. However, hundreds of new groups that arose in post-World War II Japan have resumed the longing for a divine leader; for a ruler who is a living kami.

THE SACRED RULER AND MODERN SHINTO VIEWS

The vision of the sacred ruler still lives in Shinto, although it is a deeply divisive issue. Initiatives are regularly brought before the Japanese legislature to have aspects of the imperial system restored. Yasakuni Shrine has sought tax support as a national war memorial. Appeals have been made to declare the emperor divine once again, although this issue especially divides Shinto.

Yasakuni Shinto is an artifact of prewar Shinto. It has enshrined the spirit (mitama) of thousands of war dead as kami.

It represents the part of Tennôism (imperial divinity) that took obedience to the spirit of the living kami to the extreme. It preaches obedience to a code of total loyalty. It teaches that one must be willing to die as a warrior (*bushi*) in order to become a kami, a warrior god. Branch Yasakuni shrines across Japan still practice its brand of Tennôism. It is estimated that ten percent of all Japanese still accept the tenets of nationalism and patriotism that have been championed by Yasakuni Shinto.

How Shinto solves the problems posed by the desire for a divine ruler will help to determine the shape and future of Shinto, and of Japan as well.

8

Shinto in the World Today

Where you have sincerity, there also is virtue.
Sincerity is a witness to truth.
Sincerity is the mother of knowledge.
Sincerity is a single virtue that binds
Divinity and man in one.

—Shinto Saying

S hinto enters the twenty-first century with a tradition that is rich in myth and history, ritual and liturgy, art and architecture. But how will Shinto fare in modern Japan and in a more global world? Among the problems that need to be addressed are ecological concerns, inequities in the distribution and use of the world's resources, health care, Japan's aging population, and emotional and spiritual needs. Will Shinto be an active partner in seeking solutions to these problems? What will be Shinto's reaction to racism, militarism, imperialism, and economic exploitation? Japanese popular culture grows ever more commercialized and materialistic; will Shinto address this trend and, if so, how? Can a heretofore isolated and ethnic religion take a seat at the table of interfaith dialogue and cooperation? Will Shinto find a way to share its nature-based spirituality with the rest of the world? These are some of the questions that Shinto faces today.

SHINTO'S STATUS: IS IT A "WORLD RELIGION?"

Shinto has traditionally been categorized as a local or ethnic religion, as versus a universalizing religion. It doesn't have a written code of religious law, or a theory of scriptural infallibility. It is not a monotheistic faith with a single high God. For all of these reasons and more, it appeared "primitive" in the light of standards of cultural evolution developed during the colonial period.

In the nineteenth century and early twentieth century, scholars considered indigenous religions like Shinto to be "backward" by comparison with Western religions. Since these scholars were Western by background and education, they used the religions they were most familiar with (modern Western religions) as their standard for judgment. Not surprisingly, religions other than modern Western religions did not fare well using this set of criteria. Such biases have lingering effects in the selection of religions to be included in World Religions courses and textbooks. Unfortunately, Shinto seldom makes the cut in these selections, which seems to imply that it is not a World Religion and hence not a very important religion.

Recently, however, two groups outside of Japan have advanced the argument that Shinto, along with other indigenous religions, should be studied on a par with World Religions like Christianity, Islam, and Buddhism. Some Hindus and some European Neo-Pagans are fighting to redefine "world religion" to mean an "earth-based" or *Gaia* religion. These groups intend, of course, to upset smug Western assumptions about *higher, better,* and more *advanced* in the realm of religion. Without getting involved in the particulars of these normative debates, we can take from them at least one issue worth considering: Might it not be the case that the old "Gaia" religions like Hinduism, Shinto, Native American religions, Hawaiian religion, African religion, paganism, and Neo-paganism also have values that are worthy of being shared with the rest of the world? Perhaps some of these values should even be considered normative in a world in which the list of devastated ecosystems daily casts its lengthening shadow across the future of the planet. At the very least, such religions have values that must be understood by any person of goodwill who acknowledges that we all have a responsibility toward the ground on which we stand.

SHINTO AS IMMANENT RELIGION

There are all kinds of religious signs of the divine: myths and religious narratives, theological ideas, religious acts (liturgies, private meditations), architectural and artistic symbols, books, songs, devotional objects, and so on—"anything that can be referred to as a religious object and can bear a religious meaning."[127]

The appearance of the divine involves both recognition and interpretation, and these are mediated by tradition and culture. The sacred is experienced and celebrated differently depending upon when, where, and within which faith tradition one lives. Shinto recognizes the sacred in nature, in beauty, in displays of power, in special persons, in ritual and festival, in special places; in brief, within the world. This makes it an immanent religion, as opposed to a transcendent religion. Transcendent religions recognize the sacred in something that is other-worldly—in a

FROM THE
SHINTO
TRADITION

The torii gate at Itsukushima Jinja Shrine, Miyajima
Island, Japan, dates back to the twelfth century; though
its current form was constructed in 1875. Torii, or "bird
perches," separate the sacred from the profane in the
Shinto religion.

Lion-dogs, or Shishi, traditionally stand guard outside Shinto shrines. Typically, there is one lion-dog that has its mouth open to scare off demons and another one with its mouth closed to shelter and keep in the good spirits.

This 1886 painting by Yoshitoshi Taiso, titled *Dawn Moon of the Shinto Rites*, depicts the Shinto festival known as Sanno. The festival is held in even-numbered years, alternating with the Kanda Festival, and honors the deities of the Hie Shrine in Tokyo.

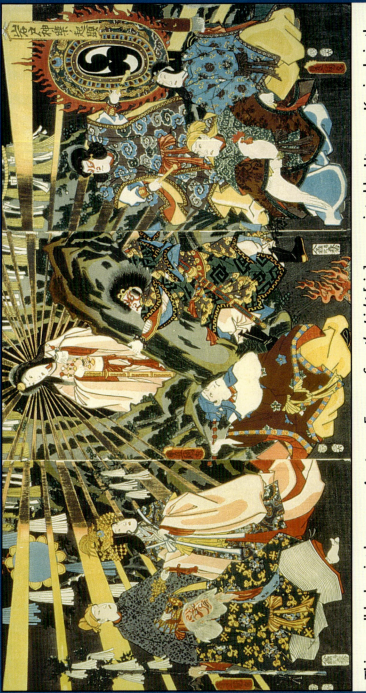

This woodblock print known as *Amaterasu Emerges from the Light* [*sic.*] was painted by Utagawa Kunisada in the nineteenth century and is housed in the Victoria and Albert Museum in London. Amaterasu is the Sun Goddess from whom Japan's imperial family is said to descend.

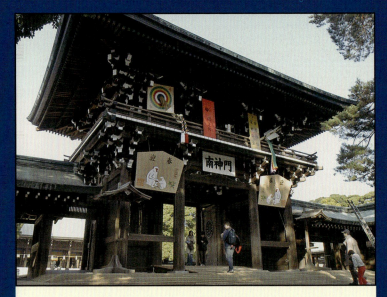

A view from the south gate of Meiji Shrine, Yoyogi Park, Tokyo, Japan. The shrine, originally built in 1920, is dedicated to the deified spirits of Emperor Meiji and his wife, "Empress Shoken," and is decorated here for New Year celebrations, during which adherents offer prayers.

Shichi-go-san is a national Japanese festival for three-, five-, and seven-year-olds, and is held every year around November 15. Children in classical dress are taken to shrines to pray for their healthy growth and seek the protection of the kami in this delicate stage of their lives.

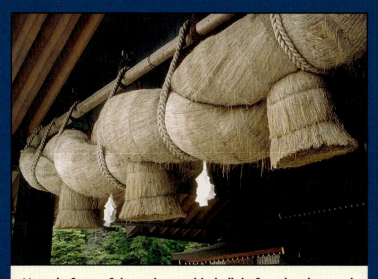

Hung in front of the main worship hall, before the altar, and across the entrance gate (torii), the presence of shimenawa is another important way to mark the demarcation between the sacred and profane. This shimenawa hangs at the Izumo Taisha Shrine, which claims to be Japan's oldest Shinto shrine, and is located near Izumo-shi, Japan.

Shinto priests prepare for a New Year ritual at Tokyo's Meiji Shrine. The end of the old year and the beginning of the new year are very important in Shinto religious practice. Millions of Japanese visit the Meiji Shrine during the first few days of the new year, when the cycle of life is renewed.

Purification rituals are an important Shinto rite; one must purify oneself before worshipping the kami because they are pure. In Japan, there are two great days of national purification—Nagoshi-no-Oharai (June 30) and Shiwasu-Oharai (December 31).

God that is above the natural world, or in a revealed text that is infallible and unchanging.

Symbols of the sacred must be negated as well as affirmed. This seems especially critical in immanent religion, where the finite most clearly serves as the locus of apprehension of the sacred. While the symbol points to the sacred, and may even participate in the sacred in some way, it is not to be identified with the sacred. There is always more to the sacred than what the symbol can convey. The symbol is less than the whole but points to the whole. Idolatry occurs when the finite claims (or is acclaimed) to be more than it is. If a symbol claims to be absolute, or if it pretends to the whole, then it is an idol. It is false. Shinto has been slow to develop ways of negating false claims of sacredness. This was especially true during periods of government control. (We will return to this problem below.)

SHINTO, ITS POSSIBILITIES—A SENSATE SPIRITUALITY

Shinto offers a fully embodied spirituality. Both individual and community are connected to the divine by sensing it within the body and in the world. This is immanent religion—here and now, in this place. The divine is experienced as beauty—unusual or not so unusual. It is experienced as unusual power and energy (ki), but any manifestation of power and energy is a reminder of the sacred. These are sensate experiences—that is, they are known through the senses and through actions. The divine is sought, cultivated, striven for, even become. As an immanent religion—one that finds the sacred within the world and within us—Shinto holds out lofty possibilities for humankind. The easiest place to see this affirmation of divine potential is in the idea of the divine ruler. He is the living symbol of human possibility and its attunement to the divine. (Since this is one of Shinto's most complex notions, we will return to this below.)

SHINTO, ITS CRISES: SURVIVAL, IDENTITY, SPIRIT
Shinto Survival in the Modern World

After World War II, scholars and politicians predicted that Shinto would not survive. Shinto not only survived—in many ways, it is flourishing. Nonetheless, Joseph Kitagawa, a leading expert in Japanese history and religion, foresees a future crisis with respect to (1) membership, (2) ability to rationally explain and transmit the faith, (3) shortage of priests, and (4) the ambiguity of its own image.[128] We will examine each of these issues in turn.

In the past, when a greater percentage of the population of Japan lived in rural areas, Shinto membership was not an issue. All persons "who resided in the vicinity of a shrine were children of the kami of that shrine and thus had an obligation to support it" (the traditional *ujiko* system).[129] Today, Japan's urban population has no clarity about membership status or relationship to a particular shrine. Many have a "weak identity" with Shinto; few are involved enough to undertake lay leadership roles or shrine governance.

Kitagawa's second point is as true today as it was when he wrote it nearly four decades ago: "... Shinto faces serious difficulties in formulating its doctrines, in propagating its faith, and in training its priests."[130] Shinto remains overly reliant on ritual and myth to transmit the faith. If Shinto is ever to be a world leader among immanent religions, it must nurture an ability to discuss the strengths and face the weaknesses of a religion that teaches that divinity is within nature.

Kitagawa's third point is also still relevant: "Equally serious is the problem of the shortage of clergy, as exemplified by the fact that there are today [1966] about 21,000 priests for 80,000 shrines."[131] While the exact numbers have changed, the percentage of shrines unattended by priests has changed very little. There is a concentration of priests at the large shrines, affording the Japanese people less opportunity to relate to a local shrine throughout a ritual year. Shinto was once an integral part of Japanese life, but today it is in some danger of becoming a mere tourist attraction, a sort of living museum piece. This may be why so many Japanese do not say that they are Shinto members, even if they visit a shrine on New Year's Day and attend at least one spring or summer Shinto festival.

Regarding the ambiguity of Shinto's image, Kitagawa notes that "the Shinto fold seems to be split between those who regard their faith as one of the religions in Japan and those who consider it a unique national faith to the extent that it warrants special recognition from the government."[132] What role should Shinto play in today's world, both in Japan and beyond? This issue is complex and important enough to warrant further discussion:

Shinto-ness

During the Meiji Restoration, Shinto was proclaimed as the national essence (kokutai) and taught as National Learning (Kokugaku). We recall that this approach to Shinto was known as State Shinto (Kokka Shinto). State Shinto was outlawed after World War II, meaning that the Japanese state could not promote religion. This threw Shinto into an identity crisis. For Shinto to assume a leadership role among indigenous and immanent religions, it must understand itself. This will require both effort and a change of attitude. Shinto must engage in self-study. It must learn how to articulate its worship, mythology, and vision of life in non-Japanese languages. (In the past this was not deemed necessary, because of the belief that no foreigner could understand Shinto and Japanese culture anyway.) Rev. Yukitaka Yamamoto was a pioneer among Shinto priests in his attempts to communicate Shinto to the world beyond Japan. Yamamoto participated in the International Association of Religious Freedom. He financed and distributed films and videos. He was responsible for various English-language publications. He also established a cultural mission called Tsubaki America in Stockton, California. The cultural mission and its house shrine moved to Granite Falls, Washington, just before Rev. Yamamoto's death in 2002.[133]

Shinto and Commercialism

The criticism of Shinto most frequently voiced by the Japanese themselves is that Shinto is only about money. This perception is quite widespread. I believe it is at least partly due to some of the issues that I have already mentioned: Shinto's failure to articulate what it is doing in its rituals, the fact that priests are poorly trained in the areas of public relations and ministry, and the lack of ability to share the Shinto vision of life with the public.

Nonetheless, it *is* hard to overlook how much business is done in the name of Shinto. The sacred is sold ever so innocently as omimori, talismans to heal and protect against hostile forces or fate. This selling of "pop-sacred" has been going on for centuries, perhaps since the beginning of Shinto's recorded history. It seems likely that a religion centered in rituals and ceremonies would be more susceptible to such commercialism than a religion based in cognitive and intellectual activities (for example, classical Confucianism always spoke against these "popular" tendencies). Shinto's image is tarnished by this commercialism.

Shinto and Idolatry

Shinto, like other immanent religions, faces the necessity of negating as well as affirming the symbol of the divine, lest it fall into idolatry. At the heart of immanent religion is the experience of the sacred in nature, in human nature, and in this world. This in and of itself does not render a religion idolatrous. What makes a religion idolatrous is treating the finite as if it were the infinite.

Paul Tillich, noted twentieth-century theologian, forcefully raised this issue. The symbol both points to and participates in the infinite, but in and of itself it is obviously finite. Care must be taken that the finite symbol is not confused with the infinite. Unless there is a way to negate the thought that the symbol is divine, a way to shear it of its divine pretensions, the symbol may be substituted for the infinite. The symbol may be verbal or visual—a statue, an institution, a holy book, or a holy person— any of these can become an idol. The symbol becomes idolatrous when it is taken literally—when what is presented to the senses and the mind here and now is confused with the infinite, which is beyond the senses and the mind. Prophets in each tradition have warned about the problem of idols, but literalism remains a potent force in religious conflicts today. Many religious problems arise when people defend their symbols as if they were divine. This is perhaps the most widespread and dangerous of the problems faced by the religions of the world today. Let's further clarify this point by focusing on a particular Shinto symbol, the sacred ruler.

Shinto's Most Sensitive Issue: A Divine Ruler

The emperor of Japan represents both the country of Japan and the Japanese people. As we have seen, Japan and its people are believed to have been created by and descended from the kami, making them divine. The belief that the emperor is divine points to the whole of that immanent divinity of which he is the representative. But are there no standards that the emperor must meet if he is to be considered divine? Can this symbol of the sacred be qualified or negated? These issues have been raised by Shinto thinkers, as we saw in chapter seven ("Sacred Ruler"), but without a satisfactory resolution.[134] Shinto needs to develop a clearer articulation of the relationship between kami-ness and its symbols of the sacred, including and especially the extraordinary symbol of the sacred ruler.

In transcendent religion, there is an infinite distance between the infinite and the finite. God is totally other than anything in creation, and for that very reason transcendent religion has very few, if any, symbols. Nothing in creation can adequately symbolize the divine. The absolute barrier between the finite and the infinite makes it easier for transcendent religion to warn against idolatry—that falsehood that deceives the worshiper, cheapens life with untruth, and undermines intellectual and spiritual development—yet even with that distance idolatry occurs.

In immanent religion, there is no absolute barrier between the infinite and the finite—the divine is not wholly other. The sacred is experienced in and through every aspect of nature, in life and all its beauty, in manifestations of power and creativity. What is experienced is a continuum, with degrees of power, beauty, and being; some of them concentrated enough to elicit awe, wonder, reverence, or fear. In this manner, immanent religion can apprehend the sacred anywhere, at any time. This is a great strength, as it reminds us that everything bears the smudges of the holy. It is only for this reason that persons (or creation itself) can be considered sacred and placed beyond the purview of solely utilitarian purposes.

On the other hand, immanent religion also has weaknesses. The consequences of Shinto's inability to speak meaningfully about idolatry were readily apparent during World War II, when only Sectarian Shinto and those elements of Shinto that incorporated a transcendent critique were able to resist being co-opted by the imperial state.

There is nothing wrong with respect, even reverence, for one's ruler. But there is no room on the planet for an infallible ruler to whom one owes total submission, obedience, and unquestioning loyalty. This imperial idea has been used to bolster totalitarian regimes throughout history, from the ancient Roman and Peruvian Empires to modern states under Hitler and Stalin. Japan has tried this idea as well, and with disastrous consequences. Shinto must revise its notion of the divine emperor to avoid repeating past mistakes. I realize that a foreigner who raises this issue will be accused of ignorance (or worse), yet it is absolutely clear to me that Shinto must address three interrelated questions.

First, what does it mean for modern Japan, no longer culturally or militarily imperial, to have a divine emperor? Second, can Shinto and Japan take responsibility for mistakes made and atrocities committed in the name of a divine emperor? There are rituals of purification in Shinto that accept responsibility for impurity and pollution; performing these rituals as an acknowledgment of past wrongs might lead Japan beyond its chronic national state of denial.[135] Third, can the symbol of the divine emperor guide the Japanese people toward acceptance of the responsibilities and possibilities of being human? The idea of a sacred ruler need not be discarded—it just needs to be reappropriated in more positive ways. To illustrate how that might happen, I offer this story about Rev. Koi Barrish, the first American Shinto priest.

Rev. Barrish was taken to a Shinto meeting at Yasakuni Shrine in Tokyo. This is the controversial shrine honoring Japan's World War II dead, including several convicted war criminals. Rev. Barrish spoke (in Japanese) about his Shinto faith and then was questioned by a skeptical audience, many of whom appeared to believe that only the Japanese could understand Shinto—certainly no American could be a Shinto priest! The first question from the audience was "Do you believe that the emperor is divine?" In response, Rev. Barrish affirmed the divinity of the emperor, and then went on to say what he meant by that: The emperor is a living reminder of what each human can become. I will now take up each of these three questions in turn and discuss it in greater detail.

First, what can the notion of a divine emperor mean in modern Japan, a country that is no longer involved in cultural or military imperialism? Is it still possible to experience the emperor as a symbol of the sacred? The question must be asked, because World War II left many Japanese with an inability to reaffirm key Shinto ideas if those ideas had played an important role in validating Japanese imperialism. Perhaps the entire imperial ideology, including the notion of the divine emperor, was the result of indoctrination. Modern Shinto is probably deeply divided over this issue, but the most conservative elements are allowed to speak for Shinto without much challenge. Speaking as an American who has seen one United States president after another exhibit clay feet, it would be good to be able to respect one's political leaders. Seeing persons of power and privilege repeatedly abuse their public trust is disillusioning—and that means disillusioning not only with respect to the character of the individuals involved, but also with respect to the political system involved. History has shown that public disenchantment is dangerous, and especially so for democracies, which are by their very nature a fragile form of government. All modern democracies, including Japan, need respected leaders. Therefore, a revered "titular ruler" would be a great cultural asset. However, this idea needs clarification: How would this ruler embody the essential characteristics of Shinto, Japan, and humanity?

Second, will Japan, and Shinto in particular, take responsibility for mistakes made and atrocities committed in the name of a divine emperor? To deny the negative incidents that occurred between 1870 and 1945 damages Japan's credibility in the eyes of the rest of the world. I received a gigantic book a few years ago, written with only one purpose in mind—to refute the idea that Japanese imperial forces carried out the Nanking massacre. The book represented the views of Shrine Shinto's most conservative members. Denial of the past includes more than just denying atrocities in China. A new Buddhist group, Rissho Kosei-kai, was the first to admit that Japan enslaved Korean "pleasure women" for its troops. This acknowledgment led the nation to ask Koreans for forgiveness. Japanese Buddhists have led pilgrimages to Southeast Asian countries to ask forgiveness of these nations; Shinto has not. The only exception was Rev. Yukitaka Yamamoto, who visited Korea as president of the International Association of Religious Freedom. Yamamoto could not wear his Shinto robes because they were offensive to the Korean people. He apologized to the Koreans for the atrocities of the war era.

Third, can the divinity of Japan's ruler become a spiritual guide for the responsibilities and possibilities of being human in a particular culture? The notion that the divine exists in nature and in humanity is found in one way or another in many of the world's religions.[136] But is there some human who is especially divine—perhaps a king or an emperor? Furthermore, is it possible to affirm a sacred ruler without falling into the twin evils of idolatry (the religious evil) and tyranny (the political evil). The idea of the sacred ruler becomes dangerous when it is mixed with an ethics of total submission and obedience. When one human is singled out as especially divine, and all others are expected to offer submission and blind obedience to that one, human freedom and responsibility are lost. This type of religious belief is often found in association with imperial regimes. Indeed, imperial rulers often intentionally cultivated, rewarded, or even created imperial religions. Jonathan Smith, a historian of religions and one of the twentieth century's towering giants in the study of religion, stated that "religion" as subservience to human and divine rulers was the creation of imperial rulers.[137]

SHINTO'S MODERN REFORMER

Reverend Yukitaka Yamamoto (1923–2002) can be considered the "Martin Luther of Shrine Shinto." While a Shinto priest (the Reverend Reuchi Shibata of the Shinto Jikko Sect) had been a participant at the 1893 World Parliament of Religions, it would be almost a full century later before a priest from mainstream Shrine Shinto would become involved in worldwide interfaith dialogue and cooperation.

Reverend Yamamoto became involved in interfaith activities after World War II, following meetings with Dr. Shinichiro Imaoka, an internationalist. Participation in such activities was an implicit criticism of Shinto's isolation and exclusivity. Reverend Yamamoto invited foreigners to his shrine, arguably one of the oldest shrines in Japan with its claim of having been founded two millennia ago. He shared Shinto's treasures with these foreigners, translating Shinto concepts from the sacred language of Japanese into Western languages. He took foreigners to Ise Grand Shrine and, by means of enormous payments, arranged for them to stand in the very spot that the representative of the emperor stands in during imperial rituals. First, the foreigner would be cleansed in a cold-water purification, misogi, at Tsubaki Grand Shrine. This was followed by a trip to Ise, the center of the Shinto ritual world. At Ise, the foreigner would participate in a ceremony so sacred that few Japanese would ever be able to have a similar experience. The purification ritual enacted at Tsubaki implied an expansion of Shinto beyond Japan and its people. Yamamoto's actions constituted a claim that persons of other nationalities could be purified and allowed to stand in Shinto's most holy space. Shinto's own rituals were used to demonstrate that the Shinto ideas of exclusivity and racial superiority were not absolute. Reverend Yamamoto would drive this point home when he convened the first All Shinto Congress at Tsubaki and Ise Grand Shrines.

Yasakuni Shinto and the Cult of Divine Dead

Yasakuni Shrine in Tokyo and its branch shrines came into existence during the Meiji Restoration. As the Meiji Restoration forged a national policy of military expansionism and Japan engaged in one war after another, her dead sons returned to be honored in a cult that deified the war dead. This made their sacrifice not only acceptable but sometimes even desirable, as in the case of the kamikaze pilots (suicide-mission soldiers). Yasakuni Shinto represents the extreme of samurai Shinto: glorifying war, obedience to military leaders, and sacrifice of one's life for country.

Yasakuni Shrine is powerful and rich, and seeks ever more influence in Japanese politics. Its theology has never been critiqued internally by Shinto's scholars (who are located in its seminaries). It is time for mainstream Shinto to reject the militaristic and chauvanistic aspects of Yasakuni Shinto in order to affirm a more peaceful Shinto, one that has no stake in Japanese racial superiority, nor in Japanese political, economic, and military dominance.

Shinto and Ecology

Shinto advertises itself as the religion of ecology. There is more image than reality to this claim at the moment. Japanese commercial interests have decimated Japan's forests. Those same corporations are now clear-cutting forests in other countries to meet Japan's insatiable appetite for wood products. In the summer of 2003, I visited Japan through a program called Semester at Sea. One of my colleagues on that trip was an ecologist. His disappointment in Shinto's claims could not have been greater. He reported that a few trees had been saved around the shrines, but massive clear-cutting had taken place elsewhere. He also reported the existence of strip-mining, polluted streams and rivers, heavy metal poisoning in harbors and the Inland Sea, and much more. He concluded that Shinto had not been able to turn its reverence for nature into true and consistent ecological practices. As the well-known modern phrase has it, Shinto was "talking the talk" (see website[138]) but not yet "walking the walk."

Perhaps his criticism is unduly harsh, but it is not far off the mark. Shinto (and other religions as well) must do more to protect nature and the planet. At least Shinto is articulating an ecological ideal, and that should provide some positive guidance for the future. Furthermore, the need to protect Shinto's image as an ecological religion, whether that image is entirely accurate or not, will make it harder for Japan to ignore the damage done to its environment. However, such ecological concern should extend to other nations' environments as well—especially those non-Japanese environments currently being exploited by Japanese firms.

Shinto and Its Possibilities

Shinto is free from state control and manipulation for the first time in its sixteen centuries of recorded history. Yet, paradoxically, its most traditional wing, the Shinto Shrine Association (Jinja Honcho), continues to seek state privileges and funding.[139]

During its fifty years of recovery following World War II, Shinto has produced only one notable prophet: the Rev. Yukitaka Yamamoto, Chief Priest of Tsubaki Grand Shrine. Yamamoto is now dead, and only time will tell whether he has left a prophetic legacy. The daily pressures involved in running a large shrine may pull Tsubaki Grand Shrine back toward the more ordinary concerns of Shinto shrines, namely, ritual and business.

Since World War II, Shrine Shinto has experienced a relatively good recovery. It currently enjoys much popular support and has even regained some of its lost prestige. Originally all forms of Shinto were blamed for teaching the militaristic ideology of Kokugaku (National Learning), but fifty years later most of the blame has been placed on State Shinto alone. The demise of State Shinto actually led to renewed relevance for Shrine Shinto.

Shinto's future also depends on how it chooses to deal with a problem that is endemic to action-centered religion, namely, how to attract young people to ritual activities and maintain their interest over time. In action-centered religion, one learns through participation in the activities of ritualized spirituality. One must be involved over a long enough period of time to "catch" the deeper meaning of the faith. However, modern life in Japan no longer supports the level of involvement that an agrarian society supported. It would help if Shrine Shinto could develop more ways of transmitting its vision of life than ritual. One possibility is the expanded use of kô groups. For centuries, kô groups have supported group activities ranging from pilgrimages to monthly purification rites (misogi). They are a likely vehicle for educating believers in their faith, especially if more young people become involved.

A New Period of Pluralism?

With the loss of national control over Shinto, this ancient religion could be entering a period of decentralized, free experimentation. In a sense, this would be a return to its history of local pluralism. Such a development would allow Shinto to experiment with new types of ministry. Rather than having only one primary focus on ritual, it might develop intellectual and mystical emphases in addition. Already Sectarian Shinto groups have developed a new emphasis on devotional religious experience. Rather than focusing on rituals, they focus on experiences of grace (unmerited personal relationship with transcendent spirit or God). A new, multidimensional Shinto should also include mystical experience (the union of the worshiper and the divine) and intellectual exploration (the use of reason and critical thinking to "unpack" mystery and challenge naïve belief). Developing all four modalities of faith (reason, intuition, emotion, and sensate functions[140]) would usher in a period of innovative growth for Shinto, and increase Shinto's relevance for all of life's stages, crises, and possibilities.

Early Shinto had a powerful symbol of female spiritual leadership in Queen Himiko, the spokesperson of the kami. Although women were not subordinated in ancient Japan, Japanese society took a decided turn toward patriarchy around the sixth century C.E. (A patriarchy is a male-centered society, one in which women occupy roles of lesser status and men occupy roles with higher status and authority.) It is unclear whether this turn of events was the result of mainland influence or native Yamato militarism, but either way, women were no longer allowed to occupy their traditional positions of power. Nonetheless, Shinto has within its own symbolism a model for sexual equality. The return of female leadership positions to mainstream Shrine Shinto would only follow what Sectarian Shinto has already accomplished. Japanese women deserve no less from their indigenous tradition.

The Discussion at Meiji

Several years ago a Japanese religious leader sought to repay my wife and I with a special gift. Although he is a Buddhist, he chose to give us a Shinto experience—a ceremony at Meiji Shrine reserved for only a few. As we signed the guest book in an inner shrine, we noted that the last person to be honored with this special ceremony was a papal representative. After the beautiful and ancient ceremony, we were ushered into a stunning reception room. Suddenly the head of Meiji Shinto seminary and several other important Shinto scholars appeared for a serious discussion: They wanted to know just how I was representing Shinto to my college students. In a conversation that lasted nearly two hours, they challenged my admiration for Tsubaki Shinto. It was not, they said, the heart of Shinto. They pointed out the beauty, wealth, and prestige of Meiji Shrine, and commented that Meiji Shinto was the true Shinto. I responded that Meiji was one center of Shinto and Tsubaki was another. I urged them to imagine a contrast between rice or village Shinto (peaceful, agrarian, welcoming, and international) and samurai Shinto (powerful, allied with the state, closed, and ethnic). This comparison of village and samurai Shinto was not meant as an insult and did not seem to be taken as one. The dialogue has continued at later conferences and meetings. I consider Tsubaki Shinto to be Shinto's conscience, its prophetic voice.

Prophetic Function in Shinto

Where is the prophetic function in Shinto? Shinto charismatics have usually been too uneducated to attain status and respect, and therefore their prophetic messages were seldom heard or followed. The exceptions to this general rule were the Shinto shamans who influenced the court with oracles from the kami.[141] Ritualized religion has long been criticized for being slow to change. Yet, Rev. Yukitaka Yamamoto demonstrated for almost half a century that Shinto's ritual of purification contains the seeds of renewal and—more importantly—creativity. But rituals cannot be done mindlessly or for profit and be instruments of renewal and creativity. We will probably need to see a new generation of Shinto priests and their shrines reach critical mass before a prophetic voice that embraces ecology and broader human ministries will be heard.[142]

Tsubaki Shinto: Model for the Future?

Rev. Yukitaka Yamamoto founded the first cultural mission to the United States—in Stockton, California. He commissioned films and video to share Shinto with the West. He wrote one of the first books about Shinto by a Shinto priest to be translated into English. He worked tirelessly in the International Association for Religious Freedom to promote interfaith and international understanding and cooperation. He brought an American student to Japan to train for the Shinto priesthood. Even though the student was not ordained, the attempt was historic. He was the first Shinto priest to receive an honorary doctorate from a prestigious Western religious institution, honoring his service to interfaith understanding and world peace. All of this has helped to change the ideas of Western scholars with respect to Shinto and Japanese culture. Textbooks no longer write Shinto off as an ethnocentric religion. It was from Tsubaki Grand Shrine that the world learned about an alternative, world-embracing form of Shinto.

Tsubaki Shinto has offered an attractive alternative to commercial exploitation of our planet. It has taught an ecologically oriented Gaia religion. It has been a traditional yet progressive form of Shinto, with courage not for war but for the evolution of the human spirit, with strength not for dominance and exploitation but for acquiring character, with determination not for personal gain but for social betterment, with direct experience not for self-worship but for the advancement of life and its possibilities.

Japan is moving away from a feudal past in which the samurai was the hero and into a new role as a leader in the Asian Century. Village Shinto is one of the world's great cultural jewels. In its pure form, it is nonexploitive, nonaggressive, experiential, social, and strengthening of mind, body, and spirit. When the world is a village, there is no more room for war, discrimination, and injustice.

Prehistoric

C. 5000 – C. 300 B.C.E. Jômon period: Fishing and hunting culture with *jômon* (cord pattern) pottery. Possible ancestor worship or veneration, totemism, continuities with Ainu (aborigines of Japan).

C. 300 B.C.E. – C.E. 250 Yayoi period: Cultural influences from Pacific islands and northeast Asian mainland; introduction of wet-rice cultivation and metals (bronze, copper, iron). Earliest Chinese reference to Japan as Kingdom of Nu or Na (C.E. 57). Shamanism evolving and helping rise of primitive kingdoms.

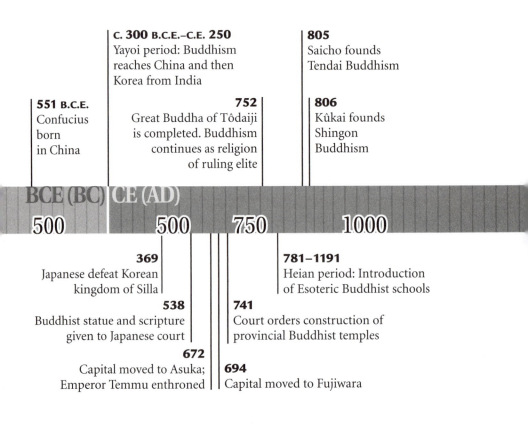

C. 300 B.C.E.–C.E. 250
Yayoi period: Buddhism reaches China and then Korea from India

805
Saicho founds Tendai Buddhism

551 B.C.E.
Confucius born in China

752
Great Buddha of Tôdaiji is completed. Buddhism continues as religion of ruling elite

806
Kûkai founds Shingon Buddhism

BCE (BC) CE (AD)

500   500   750   1000

369
Japanese defeat Korean kingdom of Silla

781–1191
Heian period: Introduction of Esoteric Buddhist schools

538
Buddhist statue and scripture given to Japanese court

741
Court orders construction of provincial Buddhist temples

672
Capital moved to Asuka; Emperor Temmu enthroned

694
Capital moved to Fujiwara

C.E. 180   Queen Himiko (or Pimiko) conquers many lesser kingdoms, ruling as shamanic queen, possibly in seclusion through her brother as active ruler.

c. 250 – c. 500   Kofun period: Burial-mound builders with much cultural contact with Paekche (Korea). Envoys exchanged with China. Known as Queenly Kingdom and as Yamatai.

Historic

c. 500 – 710   Asuka period: Yamato clan becomes imperial clan, conquers rivals, imports mainland institutions of courtly rule.

1192–1333
Kamakura period: Rise of devotional Buddhism; denominations that convert masses—Pure Land sects; Zen Buddhism arrives

1338–1573
Ashikaga or Muromachi period: Buddhist monk-warriors of Mt. Kôya killed; Shogunate attempts to weaken Buddhism

1100   1400   1700   2000

1574–1600
Azuchi-Momoyama period: Esoteric Buddhism begins to equate Buddhas and boddhisattvas with kami

1868–1945
modern period; Buddhism disestablished as state religion

1600–1867
Tokugawa period; Buddhism rejected; Shinto tolerated

593 Prince Shôtoku becomes regent and soon makes Buddhism state religion. Shinto begins to organize from local clan traditions.

604 Seventeen Injunctions (the Shotokan Constitution) promulgated.

710–781 Nara period: First permanent capital at Nara (Heijô-kyô).

712 *Kojiki* (Records of Ancient Matters) completed.

713 *Fudoki* (regional records) begun.

720 *Nihonshoki* (Chronicles of Japan) completed.

c. 766 *Manyôshû* compiled. Shinto achieves a place at court but local clans and their shrines do not become the state religion.

781–1191 Heian period: Capital moved to Nagaoka, then Kyoto. Shinto used to help state promote supremacy of Buddhism (use of Ise Grand Shrine to collect metal for Great Buddha).

791 Grand Shrine of Ise burns down.

927 *Engishiki* completed. Masses still relate more to local Shinto shrines.

1192–1333 Kamakura period: Minamoto Yoritomo becomes shogun. Capital moved to Kamakura. State uses Buddhism to control masses while attempting to control its economic and military power. Shinto is further subordinated to or amalgamated with Buddhism. Shinto remains both local and also shares some national characteristics.

1338–1573 Ashikaga or Muromachi period: Ashikaga Takauji begins Ashikaga shoguns.

1339 Publication of a book that argues for return of rule to divine emperors. Tsubaki Grand Shrine burned. Kirishitan persecuted.

1543 Arrival of Portuguese and the gun.

1549 Francis Xavier plants Roman Catholicism (*Kirishitan*) in Japan.

1574–1600 Azuchi-Momoyama period: Oda Nobunaga and Toyotomi Hideoshi are powerful shoguns, attacking all forms of military resistance, including religious armies defending shrines, temples, and churches.

1600–1867 Tokugawa period: Tokugawa Iyeyasu begins Tokugawa shogunate, first of fifteen shoguns. Period of isolation as only contact with outside world is a Dutch trading colony at Nagasaki. Shinto is tolerated. Shinto scholars begin studies of Japanese Classics, reject foreign religion (Buddhism), and seek return of divine ruler, thus laying foundation for separation from Buddhism and for becoming state religion. Appearance of first New Religions or Sectarian Shinto groups.

1853 U.S. Commodore Matthew Perry visits Japan. Unequal treaties forced on Japan.

Modern and Postmodern Shinto becomes state religion, then something beyond religion—the essence of "Japaneseness"—known as National Learning to Japanese and State Shinto by outsiders.

1868 Meiji Restoration restores rule to imperial line.

1868–1911 Meiji period: Bureaucrats and military real rulers and lead Japan into wars of colonization of Korea, Formosa, China, and Southeast Asia.

CHRONOLOGY

1912–1925   Taisho period.

1926–1989   Showa period: Emperor Hirohito.

1945   Shinto is disestablished and reorganizes as Shrine Shinto. Emperor Hirohito becomes symbolic ruler, abdicating his claim to be divine ruler. More New Religions arise. Shinto survives despite predictions that it would not.

1989– present   Heisei period: Emperor Akihito.

CHAPTER 1: Introduction

1 Rev. Yukitaka Yamamoto, *Way of the Kami, Kami No Michi*, 26.

2 *Ibid.*, 29.

3 There were earlier people in Japan—the Ainu—surviving into the present. Their religious tradition is quite distinct.

4 In the wonderful diversity of Shinto, there are several exceptions to this notion about membership, especially in the modern period. There is membership in the groups of Sectarian Shinto. Also there are functional equivalents to membership and membership rituals—so this idea may someday be replaced with a more carefully constructed one.

5 The writer who called Shinto "dualistic monism" was Nahum Stiskin, *The Looking-Glass God* (Brookline, Mass.: Autumn Press, 1972).

6 Many of these categories are no longer used, largely because they failed to accurately represent the dynamics of Eastern religions like Shinto.

7 Raymond Hammer, *Japan's Religious Ferment* (New York: Oxford University Press, 1962), 33–34. Today this kind of analysis is referred to as cultural imperialism. Its cousin, religious imperialism, is also easily recognizable.

8 William G. Aston, *Shinto: Way of the Gods* (Tokyo: Logos, 1968).

9 Will Durant, *Our Oriental Heritage* (New York: Simon & Schuster, 1963), 832.

10 *Ibid.*, 875.

11 D.T. Suzuki, *Japanese Spirituality* (Tokyo: Ministry of Education, 1972), 104.

12 One exception occurred during the modern period when belief in the divine rule of the emperor was a state doctrine and accordingly a cardinal doctrine of State Shinto. Oddly, the notions of "orthodoxy" and "heresy" were not advanced, but rather the notion of treason against the Japanese state and the person of the emperor.

13 This is why early anthropologists called Shinto *animistic* (a philosophy in which animate and inanimate things have spirits or souls that are worshipped). The concept of animism is now outdated.

14 Rudolf Otto, *Das Heilige*, translated by John W. Harvey as *The Idea of the Holy* (1923; 2d ed., Oxford: 1950).

15 We will leave open the question of whether or not Shinto's notion of *kami* ever developed a transcendent dimension—an idea of a transcendent God or gods. Note the lack of capitalization of "gods" in the English language, privileging monotheism.

16 Mircea Eliade, *The Sacred and the Profane* (New York: Harvest Books, 1959).

17 The problem of scriptural infallibility separates fundamentalists in each of these Western traditions from those who accept modern research methods. For a concise essay on this issue see William A. Grahman, "Scripture," in *Encyclopedia of Religion*, vol.13, 133–145. Also see an interesting website run by Dr. Robert Traer, http://christian-bible.com/.

18 An exception to this generalization about Shinto occurs in modern developments where monotheism is taught by some groups of Sectarian Shinto and also by some modern reformers.

19 The category of the absolute, God, ultimate concern, the infinite, etc., has been explored extensively in the modern period. One beginning point is "God" [this entry consists of five articles that discuss ideas and images of God in monotheistic traditions: God in the Hebrew Scriptures, God in the New Testament, God in Postbiblical Judaism, God in Postbiblical Christianity, and God in Islam], in *Encyclopedia of Religion*, vol. 6.

20 Examples include the Native or tribal peoples found in North America, South America, Africa, Australia, India, and nearly every other region of the globe.

21 Japanese folklore studies have advanced dramatically in the last century with only a small portion of that research making its way into English. These studies demonstrate just how interconnected Japan's culture is with other cultures in Asia. A website that shares current research in English is http://www.kokugakuin.ac.jp/.

22 Mircea Eliade, *Cosmos and History: The Myth of the Eternal Return* (Princeton: Princeton University Press, 1954).

23 Roman letters are called *Romaji* in Japanese. There are three other writing systems in "written Japanese": *Kanji* (the Chinese characters) that are not phonetic and generally monosyllabic plus two syllabic systems; *Hiragana* (for Japanese words); and *Katakana* (for foreign words). *Kanji* can be read by two pronunciation systems: *on* (its Chinese reading) and *kun* (its Japanese reading). Thus, the *Kanji* or Chinese characters for Shinto consist of two Chinese characters that are read *Shinto* in its Chinese or *on* reading and *Kami no Michi* in its Japanese or *kun* reading.

24 Nouns receive their number from the modifier instead of the addition of an ending (one kami, three kami).

25 While the imperial claim to divinity was understood in the West to have been renounced under the terms of defeat at the end of World War II, many Japanese still believe that their emperor is divine: "One cannot renounce one's true nature, even by force." There is obvious political tension between this claim and Japanese democratic ideas.

26 Quoted from Jinja Honcho, *An Outline of Shinto Teachings*, Tokyo: Jinja Honcho, 1958, 5, 6.

27 Sokyo Ono, *Shinto: the Kami Way* (Rutland, Vt. and Tokyo: Charles E. Tuttle Co., 1962).

28 The ones easiest to learn about in English are Tenri-kyô, Konkô-kyô, and Kuruzumi-kyô.

29 *Minkan Shinko* translates "folk or popular beliefs." There are numerous technical terms used for the variety of shamanic groups and their practices, some included within Shinto and some not.

30 The following resources will help to clarify this complex topic: Hori Ichiro, "Shamanism in Japan," *Japanese Journal of Religious Studies* (Vol. 2, 4, December 1975), 231–287; Carmen Blacker, *The Catalpa Bow: Shamanic Practices in Japan* (London: Allen & Unwin, 1986), 353; Joseph Kitagawa, "Prehistoric Background of Japanese Religion," *History of Religions* (Vol. 2, 2, Winter 1963), 292–328.

CHAPTER 2: Sacred Sound

31 This is almost generally true for Shinto. The major exception is how the Japanese Classics were elevated to a status that could not be questioned under State Shinto and National Learning (more in later chapters).

32 Sacred sounds will also be discussed in the chapter on sacred action.

33 I open with this discussion in order to counter the philosophical position known as reductionism, i.e., I want to demonstrate that talk about the sacred is both meaningful and necessary, and that it cannot be reduced to psychological categories or any other categories of understanding.

34 Ethnic religions are culture and language bound—they are limited to one language. It is not that worship can only be done in their own language but that the divine language is also the same as the tribe or group. Any sacred words must be in the native tongue. This is true for Hinduism (Sanskrit), Judaism (Hebrew), and Islam (Arabic). Christianity can be considered tribal when Latin became the sacred language, and few have dealt with the implications that Jesus only spoke Aramaic and used Hebrew in worship. Jesus' teachings were translated into the commercial language of the day, koine Greek. For most Christians today, the idea of God having a human language would be ridiculous.

35 Both Ise Grand Shrine and Tsubaki Grand Shrine have celebrated their two-thousand-year anniversaries, both claiming to be older than Christianity. Western historians would date both of these important shrines about C.E. 600.

36 Ann Evans, trans., *Shinto Norito: A Book of Prayers* (n.p. [Canada]: Matsuri Foundation, 2001, 138).

37 One of the words in this list (*ki*) does not appear in Shrine Shinto's *Basic Terms of Shinto* (Tokyo: Kokugakuin University, Institute for Japanese Culture and Classics, revised edition 1985). The term for emperor (*tennô*) is the Sino-Japanese reading rather than the Japanese reading that would have the divine essence of the word, its *kotodama*. The list could expand to several hundred, even including words from other types of Shinto but these six terms must suffice to illustrate the point of the sacredness believed to be *within* certain Japanese words.

38 What Japanese words (a) convey the kami-experience, (b) are pleasing to the kami, and (c) are the basic or essential concepts of Shinto? The first two items are experiential, while the third is conceptual or secondary to experience. Shintoists must discover the first two while others may discuss the third. It is obvious that we must have some working knowledge of how the word kami is used in Shinto. It is not going to be sufficient for us to translate kami as "God" or "gods" and then find that Shinto has a primitive notion of God since some trees, rocks, waterfalls, mountains, islands, and lots of other things are kami. Our job is to look for something to be experienced in each of these uses that is being called kami. What is the kami-ness that is associated with claims to having experienced kami in tree, mountain, etc.?

39 Two very reliable and readable books about Daoist (also Taoist) traditions are by Huston Smith, *Religions of Man* (New York: HarperCollins, 1958) and John Blofeld, *Secret and Sublime* (New York: E.P. Dutton). They distinguish between mystical Daoists (the "poets"),

devotional or religious Daoists (the polytheists), and the Daoist yogis (esoteric or sexual Daoism).

40 Shinto should not be classified as animism but *entheism*, becoming divine (becoming kami or kami-like). There is also the possibility that a tree or a waterfall could again become profane. Often a tree is sacred (with the shinogawa marking it off from the profane) because the kami come to it, indwelling in its branches. Once that is thought to happen, the tree can only be cut down if the kami are appeased and encouraged to allow the tree to again become ordinary or profane.

41 There is no direct evidence that early Shinto used any mind-altering plants, but hemp is still used as streamers on the sacred wands (*goshintai*) and reflects an earlier Shamanic setting.

42 Quoted from Norman Havens, "Immanent Legitimation: Reflections on the 'Kami Concept'" in Nobutaka Inoue (ed.), *Kami* (Institute for Japanese Culture and Classics, Kokugakuin University, 1998). Standard translations of this passage can be found in Ryusaku Tsunoda, Wm. Theodore deBary, and Donald Keene, comps., *Sources of Japanese Tradition* 2 vols. (New York: Columbia University Press, 1964), 21–22, and D.C. Holtom, *The National Faith of Japan: A Study in Modern Shinto* (reprinted in H. Byron Earhart, *Religion in the Japanese Experience: Sources and Interpretations* [Belmont, Calif., 1997], 10–11).

43 *Kannagara* can also be written in a combination of *kanji* and *katakana*.

44 Havens *op.cit.*, 27.

45 "Universal energy" therapy taught by the seventy-year-old Shinto shamaness, Osumi sensei. This therapy is described in Ikuko Osumi and Malcolm Ritchie, *The Shamanic Healer: The Healing World of Ikuko Osumi and the Traditional Art of Seiki-Jutsu* (London: Century, 1987).

46 The Wade-Giles transliteration of *qi* is *chi*, which without an apostrophe is pronounced in oral Mandarin Chinese as "key."

47 Helen Hardacre, *Shintô and the State: 1868–1988* (Princeton, N.J.: Princeton University Press, 1989), 40.

CHAPTER 3: Sacred Story

48 We must keep in mind the two often contradictory forces at work over the centuries within Shinto: preserving the purity of an individual shrine's traditions and consolidating Shinto into a unified tradition.

49 George M. Williams, *Handbook of Hindu Mythology* (Santa Barbara, Calif.: ABC CLIO, 2003).

50 I am currently working on a book about the core mythologies of the world's religions. When they are placed side by side, it is easier not to privilege any one of them. It is also easier to see myth as the core or foundational "sacred story" of each tradition.

51 Michael Ashkenazi's *Handbook of Japanese Mythology* (Santa Barbara, Calif.: ABC CLIO, 2003) goes a long way toward realizing this goal.

52 Basil Chamberlain's 1882 translation is available on the internet (http://www. sacred-texts.com/shi/kojiki.htm). Other English translations include those by W.G. Aston (1896) and Donald Philippi (1968).

53 Paul Varley, "[Japanese] Religious Documents," *Encyclopedia of Religion*, Vol. 7, 553–554.

54 *Ibid.* The next three books ranged through history, law, and politics.

55 *Ibid.*, 553.

56 *Ibid.*, 554.

57 *Ibid.*, 555.

58 Professor Ueda corrects English translations and argues that there are two classes of kami—those who came into being and those who were born. Kenji Ueda, "Magatsubi no Kami and Motoori Norinaga's Theology" in Nobutaka Inoue, ed., *Kami: Contemporary Papers on Japanese Religion*, Vol. 4. (Institute for Japanese Culture and Classics, 1998).

59 Divine and royal incest are seldom a problem in ancient societies as they serve to illustrate the difference between heavenly and earthly divinity and ordinary humans.

60 *Kojiki* sections 3–4.

61 Onogoro, a single island or continent, is taken to be Japan by most.

62 Some Shinto interpreters, especially of the Pacific War period, say that Hiruko is the mother of all non-Japanese.

63 *Kojiki, op.cit.*

64 This provides further evidence that the primary goals of the *Kojiki* and the *Nihonshoki* were not liturgical or religious but rather religio-political. The stories were collected to legitimate the rule of one family.

65 The *Kojiki* then states that the divine parents have given birth to fourteen islands and thirty-five kami, not counting the two misshapen first attempts.

66 This is part of the practice of giving divine origin to various loyal aristocratic families.

67 This location is especially important because the Izumo region was the last to be conquered and thus their claim to being a divine realm had to be contradicted and integrated into the Yamato ideology.

68 The birth order mentioned in this section of the *Kojiki* does not seem to fit with a later section's assertion that Susanoo is the elder brother.

69 One verse stated that Susanoo was given dominion over the Sea-Plain; a later one states that instead of ruling the land he essentially destroyed it—becoming the storm god. The Izumo were a seafaring, fishing, and hunting culture in the process of yielding to a new culture and economy based on rice and silk.

70 This is the most transparent moment in the imperial mythology where Izumo's ancestor kami representing a fishing culture resists the coming age and rule of the rice culture of the Yamato.

71 For more complete retellings of the storyline of the Classics refer to M. Anazaki, *Handbook of Japanese Mythology* (ABC CLEO, 2003); Genchi Kato, "Introduction to Shinto," in Selwyn Gurney Champion, ed., *The Eleven Religions* (New York: E.P. Dutton, Inc., 1945.), 234–241; Stuart Picken, *Shinto: Japan's spiritual roots* (Kodansha, 1980). Translators of the Classics into English include Aston, Chamberlain, and Phillipi.

72 The other *ujigami* (clan deity) of the Izumo clan is Okuninushi.

73 The Sun Buddha was just one aspect of the multifaceted Esoteric Buddhist tradition that was reaching Japan at this time. Esoteric or Tantric Buddhism was very attractive to the imperial court; it became part of the state religion in the Nara period.

74 This early mythology would not be reworked by or for the rulers of a centralized state, as seems to have happened in Israel where David consolidated the twelve tribes into a nation under one liturgical tradition having Yahweh as its deity.

75 H. Paul Varley, "[Japanese] Religious Documents," in *The Encyclopedia of Religion*, Vol. 7., 553.

76 *Ibid.*, 555.

77 The exact date of the *Manyôshû* is C.E. 759.

78 Joseph Kitagawa, *Religion in Japanese History* (New York: Columbia University Press, 1966), 16 fn. 29.

79 Ise Shinto is used historically to cover quite a range of development. It refers generally to Ise Grand Shrine as the chief shrine of Shinto as well as of the empire of Japan. Ise Shinto's claims to supremacy survived the Pacific War, the post-World War II constitution, and the restructuring of Shinto under the Shrine Association.

80 Examinations and promotions were conducted by state bureaus in the past. Today the Shrine Association (Jinja Honcho) is responsible for them.

CHAPTER 4: Sacred Action

81 A fourfold typology of religious faith and practice is being used here: actional, devotional, mystical, and cognitional. See http://www.csuchico.edu/~georgew/articles/4types.html.

82 Adapted from Tsubaki America's Newsletter from "An Insider's View of the Ceremony," by Rev. Koichi Barrish.

83 Yamamoto, *op.cit.*, 177–178.

CHAPTER 5: Sacred Space

84 It is found in the norito called the *Oharai*.

85 The word *shintai* (or *goshintai*) is the Sino-Japanese term for *mitamashiro*.

86 A combination of laxity and pressure resulting from difficult economic times led to these objects being brought to Tokyo during the medieval period and shown to raise funds. See histories by Kitagawa or D. Brown.

87 There are many other things to discover at a shrine. For instance, on one visit to Tsubaki I was entering along the Omote Sandô just behind several village women. They stopped at a notched tree and each rubbed her crotch in two joined tree trunks. They performed a fertility ritual of Folk Shinto, a place sacred to them but unknown to the priests.

CHAPTER 6: Sacred Time

88 Some say any kind of propaganda (political spin) is political mythology. But propaganda is really ideology—literalized myths. Literalized myths only mimic sacred time. There may be a great deal of tension and contradiction in genuine political myths.

89 For more about cyclical time see Mircea Eliade's *Sacred and Profane. op.cit.*

90 Keiichi Yanagawa, "The Sensation of Matsuri," in Kenji Ueda (ed.), *Matsuri: Festival and Rite in Japanese Life* (Institute for Japanese Culture and Classics, Kokugakuin University, 1988, 1997) available at http://www.kokugakuin.ac.jp/ijcc/wp/cpjr/matsuri/index.html. Quotations will refer to this article but the internet version makes accurate numbering of pages impossible.

91 Works cited by Yanagawa: Edmund Leach, "Two Essays Concerning the Symbolic Representation of Time," in *Rethinking Anthropology* (London: The Athlone Press, 1961), 124–136; Victor Turner, *Dramas, Fields, and Metaphors* (Ithaca N.Y.: Cornell University Press, 1974), in particular, Chapter 1; Kurahayashi Shôji's *Matsuri no kôzô*; Muratake Seiichi's *Kami, kyôdôtai, hôjô* (this work deals primarily with Okinawan festivals); and Sonoda Minoru's "Shukusai to seihan," which appeared in the November 2003 edition of *Shisô*.

92 William Currie, "Matsuri," in *A Hundred Things Japanese*, 20–21, quoting from Yanagawa, *op.cit.*

93 Nahum Stiskin, *The Looking-Glass God: Shinto, Yin-Yang and a Cosmology for Today* (Brookline, Mass.: Autumn Press, 1972). Stiskin invented a category of "dualistic monism" to classify the holism of Shinto for this rather odd study.

94 Quoting from Yanagawa, *op.cit.*

95 See Chapter One. Also, George M. Williams, "Experiential Phenomenology," 1979. Available at http://www.csuchico.edu/~georgew/4types/ep.html.

96 Yanagawa, *op.cit.*

97 Quoting from Yanagawa, *ibid.*

98 Kurahayashi Shôji, *Matsuri no kôzô* [The structure of matsuri] (Tokyo: Nihon Hôsô Shuppan Kyôkai 1975), see especially "Introduction." Quoted from Yanagawa, *op.cit.*

99 Minoru Sonoda, "Festival and Sacred Transgression," in Kenji Ueda (ed.), *Matsuri: Festival and Rite in Japanese Life* (Institute for Japanese Culture and Classics, Kokugakuin University, 1988, 1997) available at http://www.kokugakuin.ac.jp/ijcc/wp/cpjr/matsuri/index.html. Quotations will not contain accurate page number because of the internet version.

100 The Nippon Gakujutsu Shinkô kai, (editor and translator), *The Manyôshû* (New York: Columbia University Press, 1965), 222. Quoted from Sonoda, *op.cit.*

101 Quoted from Sonoda, *ibid.*

102 John Nelson is an important anthropologist and Shinto specialist. After graduating from my university, John taught English in Japan. He wrote to ask me how he might begin to learn about Shinto. I suggested he buy a video-camera and tape each of the festivals in the yearly cycle. That field experience became the foundation for his Ph.D. dissertation at UC-Berkeley, and for his first book, *A Year in the Life of a Shinto Shrine* (Seattle, Wash.: University of Washington Press, 1996).

103 For a fuller account in English of the Japanese New Year, see an article by S.D.B.P. in *Look Japan*, January 1984, titled "Oshogatsu: New Year in Japan— a window to the spiritual roots of modernity" which lists a vocabulary of over sixty terms that are special to the events, activities, and ceremonies of New Year. This should give an idea of how complex and developed the sequence of events actually is and how the meaning and significance of New Year has been ritualized.

CHAPTER 7: Sacred Ruler

104 A Disclaimer: This topic is almost impossible for me to treat fairly and adequately. I reside in the modern illusion that I am not ruled but am free. I probably detest rulers and any ruling class. So how can an author with such a prejudice and such illusions project himself back into a culture that identified with its ruler's very divinity and found the divine order in the very form of government that was Japan as it evolved from the Nara period (seventh and eighth centuries) through the Meiji Restoration of the emperor (nineteenth and twentieth centuries)? I will use a hybrid approach of history, phenomenology of religion, mythological studies, sociology, and political science to construct this chapter.

A Reminder: Remember the tension in Shinto between localism and national unification. This chapter will emphasize one side, national unification and the direct descent from a divine ruler— who is both emperor and high priest.

105 Japanese pronunciation or "reading" (*kun*) of the kanji is *sumera-mikoto* while the *on* or Chinese reading is *tennô*. Katakana script is usually used with *on* or Chinese readings, while hiragana is used with the *kun* or Japanese readings. Katakana is used with foreign words and also for emphasis, similar to the manner in which we use italics.

106 Delmer Brown, ed., *The Cambridge History of Japan*, Vol. 1: Ancient Japan (Cambridge: Cambridge University Press, 1993), 118, 387, 510 [588].

107 See Carmen Blacker's *The Catalpa Bow: A Study of Shamanistic Practices in Japan* (London: George Allen & Unwin Ltd., 1975) and Japanese folklore studies like *Folk Beliefs in Modern Japan* edited by Nobutaka Inoue and trans. by Norman Havens (Kokugakuin University, 1994, 1997), available at http://www.kokugakuin.ac.jp/wp/cpjr/folkbeliefs/index.html.

108 Ikuko Osumi and Malcolm Ritchie, *The Shamanic Healer: The Healing World of Ikuko Osumi and the Traditional Art of Seiki-Jutsu* (London: Century, 1987).

109 One cannot just dismiss this topic. A good starting point is the work of Charles Tart on altered states of consciousness; consciousness studies is becoming a mature discipline.

110 Max Weber's writings are extensive and of immense importance: *The Protestant Ethic and the Spirit of Capitalism, The Sociology of Religion*, etc. One starting point would be the Weberian Sociology of Religion Homepage, which has a special section on Japanese religion and government: http://www.ne.jp/asahi/moriyuki/abukuma/.

111 There is no better historical account than Delmer Brown's *The Cambridge History of Japan*, Vol. 1, Ancient Japan (Cambridge: Cambridge University Press, 1993).

112 Moriyuki Abukuma, "Weberian Sociology of Japanese Rulership and Religion." This article can be found at http://www.ne.jp/asahi/moriyuki/abukuma/.

113 *Ibid.*, footnote 28.

114 Abukuma and others see this as the beginning of worship of the sun, a religious practice that will evolve into the imperial Amaterasu cult. Prof. Harada (1978) thought that Himiko and the sun were conflated to create the Sun Goddess, foundress of the imperial line and of the nation.

115 *Ibid.*, footnotes 31–34.

116 Brown, *op.cit.,* 292.

117 The first transliteration of the Chinese character is in pinyin spelling, the second in Wade-Giles. Wade-Giles spelling is an artifact of scholarship from two centuries ago. One still finds it in older studies and a few disciplines that resist the effort it takes to learn pinyin.

118 The Izumo clan was a current military threat. The followers of Sarutahiko Ômikami seem to have been the first to be conquered.

119 Joseph Kitagawa, *Religion in Japanese History* (New York: Columbia University Press, 1966), 285.

120 This was known as the *shogunate*—a military dictatorship legitimized by the divine emperor's appointment.

121 *Ibid.*, 98.

122 Prior to this time the focus had been on local, family, or clan identities. There was a sense of class inferiority, especially for those who were not members of the warrior class, the *bushi* or *samurai*.

123 Kitagawa, *op. cit.* 284.

124 Michihito Tsushima, "Emperor and World Renewal in the New Religions: The Case of Shinsei Ryûjinkai" in *New Religions*, Contemporary Papers on Japanese Religion 2, edited by Nobutaka Inoue, trans. by Norman Havens (Originally published in 1991 by the Institute for Japanese Culture and Classics, Kokugakuin University). Available at http://www.kokugakuin.ac.jp/ijcc/wp/cpjr/newreligions/tsushima.html.

125 Tsushima, *op. cit.*, quoting a Japanese work on the *History of Oppression by the Special Higher Police in the Shôwa period*, 28, fn.18.

126 Yano preferred using the term that he most often found in the classics of (*ôkimi* or great lord).

CHAPTER 8: Shinto in the World Today

127 Robert C. Neville, *Broken Symbols*, xxii.

128 Joseph M. Kitagawa, *Religion in Japanese History* (New York: Columbia University Press, 1966), 284–288.

129 *Ibid.*, 285.

130 *Ibid.*, 286.

131 *Ibid.*, 287.

132 *Ibid.*, 288.

133 For more information on the Shinto cultural mission and shrine, see http://kannagara.org.

134 Even though the Japanese Constitution rejects imperial divinity, much of Shrine Shinto still asserts it. That is why there are perennial attempts to insert this claim into children's textbooks. Shinto seminaries do not provide opportunities for seminarians to freely debate this issue and perhaps arrive at other points of view. The road that many leaders—at the Shinto seminaries, at the imperial shrines of Meiji and Ise, and in the Shrine Association (Jinja Honcho)—are taking is to deny the negative things that happened between 1870 and 1945, to fight for special government privileges for Shinto, and to step back into the mythology (ideology) of *Kokutai* ("Japanese-ness," "national essence").

135 China, Korea, and Southeast Asia erupt each time Japanese textbooks rewrite Japan's imperial history and its military atrocities. Rites of purification can work in a similar way to confessions of sins and seeking forgiveness.

136 That the divine is in everything is a belief called "pantheism"—often characterized as "everything being divine"—although this is self-refuting. A more complex explanation of divinity's ubiquity is known as "panentheism" ("everything or all in God"). Even the great Lutheran theologian Paul Tillich espoused panentheism, saying that God was the ultimate source and ground of all being and therefore everything was within God.

137 A notion championed by Prof. Jonathan Z. Smith.

138 Website on "Shinto: Civilization of the Divine Forest"— http://jinja.or.jp/english/ci-1.html.

139 Kitagawa wrote: "The basic ambiguity of the nature of Shinto has raised many thorny issues in the post-war period. . . . redesignation of February 11, the legendary date when the first Emperor Jimmu was supposed to have founded the nation, as National Foundation Day. . . . restoring ethics courses . . . expenses for the new buildings of the Grand Shrine of Ise . . . a fund drive for the Meiji and Yasakuni shrines . . . school-sponsored visit[s] to Ise . . . " Kitagawa, *op.cit.*, 289.

140 For further discussion of these four spiritual modalities, see http://homepage.mac.com/georgewilliams2/4types/.

141 There was at least one case of an oracle bringing down a usurper of political power. It was obviously not in the interest of the ruling elite to preserve this story but, since it involved a threat to the imperial line, it got recorded in the court history.

142 Prophetic voices far more likely to usher in a period of spiritual renewal and creativity in the near future include university professors, professional writers and journalists, and Japan's New Religions.

Amaterasu Ômikami—ancestral deity of imperial house, tutelary deity of Yamato clan, Sun Goddess

aramitama, aratama—"rough" spirit; wild and primal aspect of soul

bu—martial valor

bushi—military class

Bushidô—military code

chinkon-sai—ritual to calm a disturbed spirit

Enjishiki—collection of regulations from seventh to ninth centuries, rich in *norito*

Fukko Shinto—Restoration Shinto

gohei—paper or cloth strips attached to stick and offered to *kami*

goshintai—divine symbol

haiden—worship hall

harae/harai—purification rituals

haraigushi—purification wand

hatsumôde—new year shrine visit

heiden—offering hall, closest to *honden*

Hitogami—"person-deity," result of deification of clan leader

honden—inner sanctuary, the shrine holy of holies

ichi-rei-shi-kon—four aspects of the soul (*aratama, nigitama, sakitama, kushitama*)

imi—austerities, avoidance as form of purification

jinja—shrine

Jinja Shinto—Shrine Shinto

kagura—sacred dance with musical accompaniment

kami—(1) deity, deities, gods; (2) divine, sacred, holy, extraordinary

kamidana—home altar

Kami-yo—age of the gods

kannagara —natural order; divine essence of nature

kegare—pollution

GLOSSARY

keihitsu—awe-filled sound used by priest

Kojiki—record of ancient matters

Kokka Shinto—State or National Shinto

Kokugaku—National Teachings

Kokutai—national essence

Koma-inu—"Korean dogs" at entrance to shrine

Kôshitsu Shinto—Imperial Household Shinto

kushitama—mysterious, hidden aspect of soul

Kyôha Shinto—Sectarian or Religious Shinto

matsuri—festivals

matsuri sawagi—festival uproar, referring to *matsuri's* wild and even transgressive side

matsurigoto—unity of worship and government

michi—way (Sino-Japanese is *dô* or *tô*)

miko—female shrine attendant

mikoshi—portable shrine

Minkan Shinko—Shamanic Shinto; literally "folk or popular beliefs"

misogi—purification by water

musubi—creation, birth, generation; creativity; becoming

naorai—reception after shrine ritual where participants drink *miki* with *kami*

nigimitama, **nigitama**—"benign" spirit; peaceful, refined aspect of soul

nihonjinron—Japaneseness

Niiname-sai—new rice festival

norito—prayer

Ôharae—great purification ritual

Oshôgatsu—New Year celebrations

Ryôbu Shinto—Dual Shinto

saisei itchi—unity of worship and government

sakaki—this tree's evergreen leaves are used in purification, blessings, and offerings (see **tamagushi**)

sakitama—happy, creative aspect of soul

seihan—sacred transgression, as during *matsuri*

seime—"purity" and "brightness" of heart, a necessary attitude in approaching *kami*

seimei—physical existence, what passes away at death

seinaru kanjô—sentiment of the holy

senzo —ancestors

Setsubun—bean-throwing festival

shaden—shrine buildings

Shichi-go-san—7-5-3 [year-olds] festival

shimenawa—sacred rope

shinsen—sacred food offerings

shintai—divine symbol enshrined in *honden*, the shrine holy of holies

Shukusai—festival, referring to its solemn aspects

shûkyô—modern word for "religion," literally "sect's teaching"

tama—soul or spirit, which has both good and bad aspects (see *tamashii*)

tamagushi—evergreen offering

tamashii—soul

temizu-ya—purification basin at shrine entrance

tennô—heavenly ruler, emperor

torii —distinctive shrine gateway, marking boundary between sacred and profane

tsumi—pollution of all kinds—physical, emotional, errors, calamities, sins

Tsûzoku Shinto—folk or popular Shinto; also family Shinto

ujigami—deified ancestors or tutelary deities

ujiko— parishioners

Wasshoi— chant by bearers of portable shrines

Yomi— land of the dead

BIBLIOGRAPHY

BOOKS

Ashkenazi, Michael. *Matsuri: Festivals of a Japanese Town*. Honolulu, Hawaii: University of Hawaii Press, 1993.

Aston, William. *Nihongi: Chronicles of Japan from the Earliest Times to A.D. 697*. London: George, Allen & Unwin, 1956 Reprint; Tokyo: Tuttle, 1972 Reprint.

———. *Shinto: The Way of the Gods*. London: Longmans, Green, and Co. 1905; Logos, 1968 Reprint.

Ballou, Robert Oleson. *Shinto, the Unconquered Enemy: Japan's Doctrine of Racial Superiority and World Conquest*. New York: Viking Press, 1945.

Bellah, Robert. *Tokugawa Religion*. Glencoe, Ill.: The Free Press, 1957; Boston: Beacon Press, 1970 reprint.

Blacker, Carmen. *The Catalpa Bow*. London: George Allen & Unwin Ltd., 1975.

Bremen, Jan Van. *Ceremony and Ritual in Japan: Religious Practices in an Industrialized Society*. New York and London: Routledge, 1995.

Brooker, Paul. *The Faces of Fraternalism: Nazi Germany, Fascist Italy, and Imperial Japan*. New York: Oxford University Press, 1991.

Brown, Delmer, ed. *The Cambridge History of Japan, Vol. 1: Ancient Japan*. New York: Cambridge University Press, 1993.

Bukkyo Dendo Kyokai. *The World of Shinto*. Tokyo: Bukkyo Dendo Kyokai, 1985.

Chamberlain, Basil Hall, Trans. *Kojiki*. Tokyo: Tuttle, 1982 Reprint.

Finegan, Jack. *The Archeology of World Religions: The Background of Primitivism, Zoroastrianism, Hinduism, Jainism, Buddhism, Confucianism, Taoism, Shinto, Islam and Sikhism*. Princeton, N.J.: Princeton University Press, 1952.

Fridell, Wilbur M. *Japanese Shrine Mergers, 1906–12: State Shinto Moves to the Grassroots.* Tokyo: Sophia University, 1973.

Fujisawa, Chikao. *Zen and Shinto: The Story of Japanese Philosophy.* Westport, Conn.: Greenwood Press, 1971.

Girard, René. *Violence and the Sacred.* Translated by Patrick Gregory (from *La Violence et le sacré,* 1972). Baltimore, Md.: Johns Hopkins University, 1977.

Grapard, Allan G. *The Protocol of the Gods: A Study of The Kasuga Cult in Japanese History.* Berkeley, Calif.: University of California Press, 1992.

Guth, Christine. *The Arts of Shinto.* New York: Weatherhill, 1973.

Hardacre, Helen. *Shinto and the State, 1868–1988.* Princeton, N.J.: Princeton University Press, 1989.

Herbert, Jean. *Shinto: The Fountain Head of Japan.* London: George, 1967.

Holtom, Daniel Clarence. "Shintoism" In *The Great Religions of the Modern World,* Edited By Edward J. Jurji. Princeton, N.J.: Princeton University Press, 1946, pp. 141–177.

———. *The National Faith of Japan: A Study in Modern Shinto.* New York: Paragon Book Reprint Corp., 1965.

Honda, H.H., Trans. *Manyôshû.* Tokyo: Hokuseido Press, 1967.

Iro, Nobuo. "Shinto Architecture." *Kodansha Encyclopaedia of Japan.* Tokyo: Kodansha, 1983, pp. 132–134.

Jinja Honcho. *Basic Terms of Shinto.* Tokyo: Jinja Honcho, 1958.

———. *Jinja Shinto Shrines and Festivals.* Tokyo: Jinja Honcho, 1970.

———. *An Outline of Shinto Teachings.* Tokyo: Jinja Honcho, 1958.

Kanda, Christine Guth. *Shinzo: Hachiman Imagery and Its Development.* Cambridge, Mass.: Council On East Asian Studies, Harvard University, 1985 (distributed by Harvard University Press).

BIBLIOGRAPHY

Kato, Genchi. *A Study of Shinto: The Religion of the Japanese Nation.* Tokyo: Meiji Japan Society, 1926. Reprinted by London: Curzon Press, 1971.

———. *A Historical Study of the Religious Development of Shintô.* Trans. by Shoyu Hanayama. Tokyo: Ministry of Education, 1973.

Kitagawa, Joseph. *Religion in Japanese History.* New York: Columbia University Press, 1966.

Kiyota, Minoru. *Gedatsukai, Its Theory and Practice: A Study of a Shinto-Buddhist Syncretic School in Contemporary Japan.* Los Angeles: Buddhist Books International, 1982.

Mason, Joseph Warren. *The Meaning of Shinto: The Primeval Foundation of Creative Spirit in Modern Japan.* 1935. Port Washington, N.Y.: Kennikat Press Inc., 1967.

———. *The Spirit of Shinto Mythology.* Tokyo: Fuzambo, 1939.

Matsunaga, Alica. *The Buddhist Philosophy of Assimilation: The Historical Development of the Honji-Suijaku Theory.* Tokyo: Sophia University; Rutland, Vt.: C.E. Tuttle Co., 1969.

Nelson, John K. *A Year in the Life of a Shinto Shrine.* Seattle, Wash.: University of Washington Press, 1996.

Ono, Sokyo. *Shinto: The Kami Wa.* Rutland, Vt.: Charles E. Tuttle, 1962.

Osumi, Ikuko, and Malcolm Ritchie. *The Shamanic Healer: The Healing World of Ikuko Osumi and the Traditional Art of Seiki-Jutsu.* London: Century, 1987.

Philippi, Donald L., trans. and ed. *Kojiki.* Tokyo: University of Tokyo Press, 1968.

Picken, Stuart D.B. *Handbook of Shinto.* Stockton, Calif.: Tsubaki America, 1987.

———. "Shinto and the Beginnings of Modernization in Japan." *Transactions of the International Conference of Orientalists in Japan* 22 (1977): pp. 37–43.

———. *Shinto, Japan's Spiritual Roots.* Tokyo: Kodansha International Ltd., 1980 (distributed in the U.S. through Harper & Row, 1980).

Ponsonby-Fane, Richard Arthur Brabazon. *Studies in Shinto and Shrines, Papers Selected from the Works of the Late R.A.B. Ponsonby-Fane.* Kyoto, Japan: Ponsonby Memorial Society, 1962.

Sakamaki, Shunzo. "Shinto: Japanese Ethnocentrism" in *The Japanese Mind*, edited by Charles Moore. Honolulu, Hawaii: University of Hawaii Press, 1967, pp. 24–33.

Sansom, Sir George. *A Short Cultural History.* New York.: D. Appleton-Century, 1931.

———. *History of Japan.* 3 Volumes. Palo Alto, Calif.: Stanford University Press, 1958–1963.

Sharma, Arvind, and Katherine Young (eds.). *Women in World Religions.* Albany, N.Y.: State University of New York Press, 1994.

Smith, Jonathan Z. *Imagining Religion: From Babylon to Jamestown.* Chicago: University of Chicago Press, 1982.

Spae, Joseph John. *Shinto Man.* Tokyo: Oriens Institute for Religious Research, 1972.

Stiskin, Menahum Nahum. *The Looking-Glass God: Shinto, Yin-Yang and a Cosmology for Today.* New York: Autumn Press, 1972 (distributed By Weatherhill).

Stoesz, Willis. *Kurozumi Shinto: An American Dialogue.* Chambersburg, Pa.: Anima Books, 1989.

Supreme Commander for the Allied Powers. *Religions in Japan: Buddhism, Shinto, Christianity.* 1948; Rutland, Vt.: C.E. Tuttle Co., 1955 reprint.

BIBLIOGRAPHY

Tsunoda, Ryusaku, William Theodore De Bary, and Donald Keene. *Sources of the Japanese Tradition.* New York: Columbia University Press, 1958.

Tyler, Royall. *The Miracles of the Kasuga Deity.* New York: Columbia University Press, 1990.

Underwood, Alfred Clair. *Shintoism: The Indigenous Religion of Japan.* London: The Epworth Press, 1934.

Watanabe, Yasutada. *Shinto Art: Ise and Izumo Shrine.* New York and Tokyo: Weatherhill, 1974.

Webmeyer, Ann, Trans. *Kojiki-Den [Motoori Norinaga], Book 1.* East Asia Series, No. 87. Ithaca, N.Y.: Cornell University Press, 1997.

Yamamoto, Rev. Yukitaka. *Kami No Michi: Way of the Kami.* Stockton, Calif.: Tsubaki America, 1985, Second Edition 1993.

Young, Arthur Morgan. *The Rise of a Pagan State: Japan's Religious Background.* New York: William Morrow & Co., 1939.

AUDIO/VIDEO

Harich-Schneider, Eta. *Japan (V); Shinto Music.* Barenreiter Musicaphon, 1960. (Audio)

Hirai, Naofusa. *Modern Shinto.* 1966. (Video)

Inagaki, Hiroshi. *Chûshingura.* Tohoscope, 1962. (Video)

Kanda, Rev. Shigeo. *Shinto Multimedia Dictionary.* America Academy Of Religion. (CD)

Kurosawa, Akira. *Those Who Tread on the Tiger's Tail* [Tora No Ofumu Otokotachi]. Academy Ratio, 1945. (Video)

Ono, Motonori. *Shinto.* (Slide Tape)

Shinomia. *Misogi.* Tsubaki Grand Shrine, Japan. (Video)

Shinto: Nature, Gods, and Man in Japan. Japan Society Films, 1970. (Video)

Tokugawa, Muneyoshi. *The Divine Renewal of Ise Shine, the 60th Shikinen Sengu, Periodic Ceremony of the Moving of the Shrine, October 1973.* Geiken Productions, 1980. (Video)

Williams, George. *Series on Shinto Rituals and Festivals.* Tsubaki America, 1990–1995, 2004.

FURTHER READING—WEBSITES

Cyber Shrine
http://www.kiku.com/electric_samurai/cyber_shrine/

Encyclopedia Mythica
http://www.pantheon.org/areas/mythology/asia/japanese/articles.html

Institute for Japanese Culture and Classics, Kokugakuin University
http://www.kokugakuin.ac.jp/ijcc/wp/

Japanese Gods and Goddesses
http://www.artelino.com/articles/japanese_gods_and_goddesses.asp
http://www.artelino.com/articles/japanese_mythology .asp

Japanese Myth
http://www.st.rim.or.jp/~cycle/myrefe.html

Nihongo.org
http://www.nihongo.org/english/

Sacred Texts: Shinto
http://www.sacred-texts.com/shi/

Shinto Online Network Association
http://www.jinja.or.jp/english/index.html

Tsubaki America. Kannagara Shrine
http://www.kannagara.org

Tsubaki Grand Shrine
http://www.cjn.or.jp/tsubaki/ (Japanese)

INDEX

INDEX

and Sectarian Shinto, 20
and Shamanic Shinto, 21, 26
and *shen/shin,* 16, 27, 29–30, 32
and Shrine Shinto, 19
and shrines, 74
and visiting shrines, 77
kami no michi, 15–17
kamidana (god shelf), 22, 60, 76, 106, 107
kamikaze (divine wind), 121
kamikaze pilots (suicide-mission soldiers), 140
kami-ki (potential experience of divine power), 67
Kami-yo (age of the *kami*), 47–50, 94–95, 125
kannagara (divinely), 28, 33
Kannagara Shrine, 25
Kannamae-sai (harvest festival), 109
kan-na-zuki (October), 109
kannushi (priest), 60, 61
kanreki (age sixty-one), 107
kataribe (oral traditions), 26–27
keihitsu (invocations), 26, 60–61
kensen (act of offering food to *kami*), 59, 60, 61, 63, 84, 90
kessai (purification ceremony), 65–66
ki (power), 11, 28, 30, 32, 33–34, 56, 61, 68, 70, 131
kimi (great ruler), 112
kimigayo (Japanese national anthem), 112
kimono, 106
Kitagawa, Joseph, 132–133
kô groups, 85, 142
Kogiki, 34
Kogoshui (Gleanings from Ancient Stories), 52
Koi-no-bori (boys' festival), 108
Kojiki, 26, 30, 32, 41, 42, 44, 45, 46, 47, 48, 51, 66, 67, 80, 83, 85, 93, 112, 118, 119, 121, 124
Kojiki-den (Norinaga Motoori), 31–32

Koko, 46
Kokugaku (patriotism or National Learning), 118, 120, 123, 141
Kokugakuin University, 33
Kokuryuon-no-Okami (*kami* of water, life, and *ki*), 69
Kokutai (national essence), 120, 124, 133
Kokutai no Hongi, 120
Koma-inu/Shishi-koma-inu (Korean lion-dogs), 80
kon (soul), 68
Konomoto, 49
Konryu Myôjin, 67, 85
konusa (small branch of *sakaki* tree or other evergreen), 65
Korea, 81, 122, 138
koshogatsu (Little New Year), 105
kotodama (sacred word power), 25, 26, 27, 72
kun reading, 29
Kunimi, Mount, 89
Kunitokotachi-no-Mikoto (earthly *kami*), 69

language. *See* sacred sound

MacArthur, Douglas, 122
Mahâkâla, 81
Manyôshû (Collection of a Myriad Leaves), 52–54, 101
marriage, 106
matsuri (festivals), 5, 6, 15, 53, 93, 97–110, 101
matsuri sawagi (festival uproar), 101
matsurigoto (government), 36
Matsushita, Konosuke, 86
mei (life), 68
Meiji Era, 120
Meiji Restoration, 118, 120, 133, 140
Meiji Shrine, 143
membership, 4–6, 132
michihiko (leader), 69, 70

INDEX

pluralism, 142–143
pollution. *See tsumi*
power. *See ki*
priests, 11, 20, 21, 26, 44, 57, 59,
  60–61, 65–66, 84, 105, 132,
  134, 144.
  See also Yamamoto, Yukitaka
prophetic function, 144
Protestantism, 6, 57
purification. *See harai*

qi (breath, energy, power), 33
Qur'an, 11

reason, 142
rei (spirit), 68
Reisho-an (traditional tea house), 86
Rei-tai-sai (festival associated with
  Sarutuhiko Okami), 109
relative truth, 7, 10, 13.
  See also sacred sound; sacred story
Religious Shinto. *See* Sectarian
  Shinto
rice, 52, 81, 84, 103–104, 105–106,
  108, 110
rice Shinto, 143
*Rin-Pyo-To-Sha-Kai-Zin-Retsu-
  Zai-Zen*, 70
rituals, 5, 6, 14, 19, 24–25, 34, 50,
  55–72, 84, 96, 134, 141, 142, 144.
  See also misogi-harae
Rissho Kosei-kai, 138
rulers. *See Tennô*
Russia, and Russo-Japanese War, 122
Russo-Japanese War, 122

sacred action, 5, 6, 14, 19, 24–25, 34,
  55–72, 96, 134
sacred community, 14, 15
sacred music, 60
sacred ruler, 15, 17, 111–127, 131,
  135–139
sacred sound, 23–36, 57, 133
sacred space, 73–91.
  See also shrines

sacred story, 6, 14, 26, 29–30, 32, 34,
  35, 37–54, 57, 96, 101.
  See also Japanese Classics
sacred time, 7, 10, 14–15, 92–110
sacred words, 24, 25–26, 57
sai (worship), 36
saisei itchi (unity of worship and
  government), 36
Saisyu (master of ceremony), 61
sakaki (evergreen) branch, 50, 65,
  90
Sakashio (purifying salt), 70
sake (rice wine), 59, 84, 85, 90
samurai Shinto, 140, 143
samurai warriors, 17, 145
Sanshuden (Guest House), 89
Sarutahiko Okami (chief of earthly
  kami), 50, 51, 69, 80, 81–83, 85,
  96, 109, 118
scholarship, biased, 7–9
seclusion, 100
Sectarian Shinto (Kyôha Shinto), 17,
  20, 74, 123–126, 136, 142, 143
sei (government), 36
seihan (sacred transgression), 101
Seijin-no-hi (coming-of-age day),
  106
sensate spirituality, 131
Setsubun (day before official beginning of spring), 106–107
sexual equality, 142–143
Shamanic Shinto (*Minkan Shinto*),
  17, 20–21, 22, 26, 30–31, 33–34,
  43, 57, 115–117, 144
Shamushô, 84
Shen Dao (religious Daoism), 29
shen/shin, 16, 27, 29–30, 32
Shichi-go-san (festival for three-,
  five-, and seven-year-olds), 109
shimenawa (sacred rope), 74, 76, 90
shinenkai (New Year's parties), 105
Shinsei Ryûjinkai, 123–126
shinsen (food offerings), 59, 60, 61,
  63, 84, 90
"Shinto," as expressing unity, 15–17

INDEX

Page:

75, 79, 81–83, 86–89, 91: Courtesy George Williams

B: © Dallas & John Heaton/CORBIS

C: © Sakamoto Photo Research Library/CORBIS

D: © Asian Art & Archaeology, Inc./CORBIS

E: © Victoria & Albert Museum, London/Art Resource, NY

F: (top) Associated Press, AP/Chiaki Tsukumo

F: (bottom) Associated Press, AP/European Press Photo Agency

G: (top) © Paul A. Berry/CORBIS

G: (bottom) © Reuters/CORBIS

H: © Chris Lisle/CORBIS

Cover: © John Dakers; Eye Ubiquitous/CORBIS

CONTRIBUTORS

GEORGE M. WILLIAMS was awarded a Ph.D. from the University of Iowa in 1972, specializing in religion in modern India. Williams taught one year at Newton College of the Sacred Heart, Boston, before going to California State University, Chico, in the fall of 1972, joining its newly formed Department of Religious Studies.

His work with Buddhist and Shinto groups has taken him to Japan twenty-two times and he has produced three videos on aspects of Buddhism and seven on Shinto. Williams was fortunate enough to know personally some of the major religious leaders of twentieth-century Japan, including Dr. Shinichiro Imaoka, President Nikkyo Niwano of Rissho Kosei-kai, Rev. Dr. Yukitaka Yamamoto, and many others. He previously wrote *Handbook of Hindu Mythology* (2002) and is currently working on a dual study of comparative spirituality—from ideal and highly critical perspectives.

ANN MARIE B. BAHR is professor of religious studies at South Dakota State University. Her areas of teaching, research, and writing include World Religions, New Testament, Religion in American Culture, and the Middle East. Her articles have appeared in *Annual Editions: World Religions 03/04* (Guilford, Conn.: McGraw-Hill, 2003); *The Journal of Ecumenical Studies*; and *Covenant for a New Creation: Ethics, Religion and Public Policy* (Maryknoll, N.Y.: Orbis, 1991). Since 1999, she has authored a weekly newspaper column which analyzes the cultural significance of religious holidays. She has also served as president of the Upper Midwest Region of the American Academy of Religion.

MARTIN E. MARTY, an ordained minister in the Evangelical Lutheran Church in America, is the Fairfax M. Cone Distinguished Service Professor Emeritus at the University of Chicago Divinity School, where he taught for thirty-five years. Marty has served as president of the American Academy of Religion, the American Society of Church History, and the American Catholic Historical Association, and was also a member of two U.S. presidential commissions. He is currently Senior Regent at St. Olaf College in Northfield, Minnesota. Marty has written more than fifty books, including the three-volume *Modern American Religion* (University of Chicago Press). His book *Righteous Empire* was a recipient of the National Book Award.